The
Little Church
of Mended People

Edited by Stewart French

authorHOUSE®

AuthorHouse™ UK Ltd.
500 Avebury Boulevard
Central Milton Keynes, MK9 2BE
www.authorhouse.co.uk
Phone: 08001974150

Published by AuthorHouse 9/21/2012

ISBN: 978-1-4772-2187-7 (sc)
ISBN: 978-1-4772-2188-4 (e)

Edited by Stewart French

This book is printed on acid-free paper.

"Little Church of Mended People"

Next to "The Rose Inn", at the junction of Ulley Road and Faversham Road in Ashford, Kent, meets a church with a history of ministry to the people of Kennington which stretches back more than a century. Most of its current members are in their forties and fifties, so for them the knowledge that God has brought His church through such varied times is a reassurance, rather than a living memory.

The first church was on the present site, but it was a wooden building with pews and a coke stove for heat. In 1913 the church was extended to provide a classroom and a kitchen. In 1970 there was a merger of the United Reformed (Congregational) Churches and the Methodist Church in Ashford, with the consequent sale of one of the premises, some of the proceeds of which went into building a new church at Kennington, on the site of the old one.

Later an extension was built in December 1979. This is now the church lounge. From 1980 there were regular morning and evening services, though in the last few years the evening service has no longer been held. The church grew and developed. In May 1987 several of the members of the church felt led to start another fellowship elsewhere in Kennington. Although this was a very sad time for the church, for a few months housegroups continued meet, involving both fellowships, but by July even these had separated.

The church has, however, continued to develop and explore new areas of ministry. Over the subsequent years we have organised a Holiday club for local children and have supported members on missions to Romania, Kosova and to a local prison, and we have had three former members becoming ordained within the United Reformed or Methodist Churches.

Over the last 10 years new members have joined us and others have gone to support other churches. A number have become preachers or worship leaders. The church has a reputation for being a loving and encouraging fellowship, but also a bit radical in its approach to worship. This book contains just a few of the stories of past and present members of this "Little Church of Mended People".

Foreword by Rev. Dr. Philip Luscombe

'An army of ordinary people.' I'm not sure whether Dave Bilbrough's song naturally fits together with the second letter of Peter: 'Once you were no people, but now you are the people of God.' The two phrases flashed into my mind as I read through the stories gathered together in this booklet. The first impression on reading the stories people have to tell about their contact with Kennington Church is an extraordinary one: lives changed; broken people remade into new strength; friendships formed and marriages made.

I have known one or two of the people who tell their stories for many years, and am only now getting to know others, but there is a long standing pattern here of Kennington playing an important part in the lives of so many people, and an important part in their decision to offer Christian service: as ordained ministers, lay preachers and in a variety of roles within the Church.

For years Kennington has been a community that has changed women and men and sent them out to serve the Church. This has never been a large Christian community but it has selflessly helped to enrich so many others.

At its best the Church can welcome ordinary, wounded people and make them into the people that God knows they really are. For me the turning point of the parable of the Prodigal Son is the thought that comes to the younger son at the depth of his degradation: 'And when he came to himself.' All the foolishness and wildness is not the real person who, it sometimes seems, only God can see clearly. God sees our potential and can take us out of our hurt isolation and mould us not only into complete individuals, but also into God's people:

'But you are a chosen race, a royal priesthood, a holy nation, God's own people, in order that you may proclaim the mighty acts of Him who called you out of darkness into His marvellous light. Once you were not a people, but now you are God's people; once you had not received mercy, but now you have received mercy.' (I Peter 2.9-10).

These stories give us the concrete details of how this continues to happen – quietly, day by day – in our own communities.

The stories told here then are special, unique and to be celebrated. But perhaps what is most important about them is that they remind us that stories like this don't need to be unusual: 'An army of ordinary people.'

One of the most powerful modern writers on ethics is very honest about himself. Stanley Hauerwas says that he has written much about Christian community, but never found it easy to live in community. But eventually, says Hauerwas, he realised that, 'being formed in the Christian virtues is not a matter of choosing the right community, but rather acknowledging the fact that Christ is revealed in those…' At this point almost every reader looks up from the book and thinks: who is he talking about? The great heroes of our faith? Those who are conspicuously filled with the Spirit? Those who set an example in times of trouble? Who work with the poor? Who suffer for their faith?

No, Hauerwas continues, 'Being formed in the Christian virtues is not a matter of choosing the right community, but rather acknowledging the fact that Christ is revealed in those with whom we have the great good fortune to be stuck.'

So, as you read these stories, give thanks for everything that is special and surprising and unique about them. But also look around you and give thanks that in God's own way He is waiting to repeat those stories – not repeat; every person is special – God is waiting to tell a new set of stories in the lives of our communities now.

Revd Dr Philip Luscombe

Minister, South Kent Circuit
May 2012

Index of Testimonies

Tricia Davis ═══════════

I arrived at Kennington Church in January 1983 and moved on just over two and a half years later, a completely transformed human being!

This was a church that welcomed me into the family on my first visit as a homesick young woman as I started my working life after university. I had visited another church nearby my on first Sunday in Kennington and sat tearfully in a pew with no one speaking to me. My landlady told me there was another church up the road (the URC/Methodist church) so that is where I went the following Sunday and the warm, friendly reception I received made a huge difference to my new life in the Ashford area.

I was invited to people's homes for coffee and for meals. I began to take part in church life – helping out in dramas, church meetings etc. The minister, Rev Richard Davis, visited me in my flat on more than one occasion and suggested I might like to become a church member. He also invited me to a video teaching series due to be held in someone's home one Friday evening/Saturday – it was to be 8 hours of teaching. I was not keen to go, but felt obliged as

Richard had been so kind to me. I mentioned at work that I was going to have to endure this event!

It was, however, an amazing two days – Richard picked me up after work on the Friday evening and we went to the home of John and Deborah Pike in Bethersden. There were a lot of church folk there; I think some of us sat on the floor. The videos began (Dynamic Christian Living by Selwyn Hughes and Trevor Partridge) and in the first half an hour of teaching I discovered what the Christian message really meant – how it was something that encompassed your whole life, not just Sunday mornings. I felt like I had fallen in love with Jesus and went home on a high – prayed (for the first time really) most of the night – chatting away to God – a whole new world opened up to me. The Saturday was fantastic – I lapped up all the teaching. I became a church member on the Sunday and felt the presence of the Holy Spirit flow into my body and my life.

Lots of wonderful Christian people opened up their lives to me and welcomed me even further into the Christian family: Janet Dray, May Francis, Stewart and Gwen French and many more. My 'first' Christmas soon after that was the most meaningful Christmas I have ever experienced.

As I walked through this new life I realised that I had not only fallen in love with Jesus, but also with the minister, Richard! I thought probably that was like fancying your doctor so was out of bounds, but I couldn't help knocking on the manse door from time to time asking Biblical questions; I even invited Richard round to my flat for a cup of tea after his busy Christmas visiting schedule. He came and whilst looking up words together in a dictionary we realised that our feelings for each other were mutual. My life felt like a wonderful fairy tale.

The church nurtured me as a young Christian. I had an encouraging prayer partner in Isabel Elliott. I attended mid week praise meetings and nights of prayer; I learned about fasting and I thoroughly enjoyed a week at the Christian holiday conference 'Spring Harvest'. I was part of a Bible study group and led a meeting on Mark chapter 1. I took my first ever service of worship at Kennington one August evening preaching on "New wine in old wine skins" and was challenged by several people including May Collins about whether I might have a call to enter the ministry. The church even paid to send me to a Christian Training Centre at Roffey Place near Horsham in Sussex. I learned a lot in the six months I was there, which stood me in good stead for the next phase in my life - marriage.

Richard and I were married in April 1985, a year and a quarter after that 'first' Christmas, at Bank Street URC/ Methodist church by Rev John Lakin. I would have loved to have been married at Kennington but we realised a larger venue would be required as so many people wanted to join with us on our special day. It was a truly wonderful occasion which I can still remember today as if it had only happened last week!

Within a few months my time in Kennington came to an end as Richard was called to a new challenge and we moved from Ashford to Basildon in Essex. It was sad to leave so many good friends behind but I shall never forget Kennington since my life was completely changed and from there I began my adventure of faith. I have followed Jesus ever since – a journey that has taken Richard and me from Basildon to Hemel Hempstead to Potterspury to Milton Keynes to Brackley to Morecambe and soon to Eastham on the Wirral. A journey that has included the gift of two beautiful children, Jonathan and Danielle who are now twenty three years old. A journey that has included a call for me to enter the ministry!

God is good! Through ups and downs Richard and I have known God's love for us. The children were a miracle, given the medical opinion that we would never have children. Later the anguish we felt as our daughter Stephanie was stillborn meant we had to lean on Jesus more than ever before. Joy as the children grew up, went to university and now live independent lives: Jonathan married to Rachel, living in Brighton and working for a church and Danielle fulfilling her dream of living and working in London. Illness has been a challenge for us - Richard has Multiple Sclerosis and has to live his life from a wheelchair. I had over five years of ME/Chronic Fatigue Syndrome. However these trials are chances for us to grow closer to God and that is what we try to do.

I am very excited that a new phase of life is now opening up for us. I believe that I have work to do still in my role at St. David's URC, Eastham and as a 'Fresh Expressions' minister in the Mersey Synod and look forward to beginning that later this year. I am so grateful that Kennington Church helped me set off on a life of such joy and fulfilment. Jesus is Lord and I wish everyone could know that.

Bill Pearson

When I was a child I was lucky to have loving and caring parents. I was the eldest of five children: four boys and the youngest who was a girl. My parents were strict, my father being an ex-Regimental Provost Sergeant, but very loving and we were all made to go to Sunday School every week.

During this time I enjoyed my visits to these classes, but was not sure what they were all about. If my parents had not insisted we attend regularly I would probably have gone to only a few of them. My parents were not church goers, but felt we needed the spiritual input from these classes.

The first time that I really began to feel the benefits from this education was when I was in my teens. I was an apprentice plumber and I was extremely worried about something, (I cannot remember what it was) but was so upset, I remembered back to my childhood and the instructions that one should always pray when a crisis happened.

That particular day I knelt in the shell of this house in which I was working and asked the Lord to help me. It was just as if I was talking to someone on the phone. I jumped up after this, in case one of the other building workers came and saw me. However, I felt better and my worries left me. I then forgot about what I had done, but to this day remember the peace that I received.

I still did not fully believe in the teachings of the Bible: after serving my apprenticeship as a plumber, I went into nursing and eventually became a qualified State Registered Nurse.

During my childhood I had needed to go into hospital for an operation or two and loved my time there. As a result of this, during my later teens, I did voluntary work in a local hospital where I made many friends. During this time, on one of my shifts there, I saw a seriously ill man who was dying and one day a Catholic priest came to give him the last rites. I thought that this was terrible, thinking that if the man saw a priest giving the last rites he would be absolutely mortified.

The next day that man died but his face looked twenty years younger and the stress lines had gone from his face. This taught me to realise that he had faith and that seeing the priest, and receiving his blessing, was a wonderful blessing to him.

During my nursing career and just after qualifying I met my wife to be and after courting her I was blessed to obtain her hand in marriage. I was taken to see her parents and dutifully asked her father for permission to marry his daughter. This was granted. It turned out to be the real start in my journey towards the Lord. Both Jill's parents were strong Christians and every Sunday I went to church with them and gradually began to understand what Christianity was all about. They were beautiful people and I learned a lot from them.

Both they and my wife (I found out later) were praying for me, and now I am extremely grateful for their prayers.

Over the years I gradually got promotion in my job and travelled to several parts of the UK and eventually became a Nursing Officer. The first was in charge of a three hundred and fifty bed General hospital on night duty, before transferring to Kent, in charge of a two hundred and fifty bed Geriatric hospital on days.

During my time in management in several hospitals I was fortunate to be able to bring my knowledge of God to help both patients and staff in many of the places that I have worked.

In the latter stages of my working life I left the Health Service and became the Manager of several homes for the elderly mentally infirm (Alzheimer) patients. During this time I was able to witness to many patients and relatives, especially relatives, as this is an extremely stressful time for them and I hope that my advice and prayers for them helped to bring them peace.

Finally, the many friends that I have met at Kennington Church have also helped me on my way to enlightenment and though I am not perfect by any means, with their help I have moved closer to the Lord.

Jill Pearson, Mavis and Rad Rodriguez

"Count your blessings"

My belief in God has been instilled in me through my loving family, particularly my maternal grandmother. This belief has been strengthened over the years by the telling and re-telling of what has happened in the past to my family and in the experiences of my life in the past up to the present.

One event which stands out happened during the war with Japan in Burma in 1942. My mother had moved from Rangoon to Maymyo in the north of Burma to avoid the conflict in the capital. She was accompanied by her parents, as my father had joined the army to fight for 'King and Country'.

I was born on the 11th January 1942 and, as the war was escalating, they decided to flee to India. My mother had told my father that they would be going to Bangalore, staying with my grandmother's aunt and uncle and gave him their address. Unfortunately due to a change in circumstances as a result of the uncle's ill health, they could not go to Bangalore, so they had to make other arrangements. My mother wrote and told this to my father, but as the army was on the move and then on the trek out of Burma, he did not receive the letter.

Many months later they were now living in Shimla, in the Himalayas. My mother was convinced that my father had been killed as she had not heard from him. She was advised to put an article in the newspaper, asking if anyone knew the whereabouts of Radford Rodriguez and gave his army details and her details. She received several replies from people saying that the last time they had seen my father he had been alive and well. In the meantime my father had reached India with the army but their Commanding Officer ordered that they make camp away from the nearest town for a time of rest and recreation. This was to build up the stamina and morale of the men before they mixed with the general population as they were completely demoralised in defeat.

One day Dad had taken part in a football competition, his team had played their match and he was watching the next match, sitting on a bench. It was very hot day with a little wind. He noticed a little scrap of newspaper being blown by the wind across the ground. He was too tired to get up and pick it up but the wind brought the paper to him and, when he picked it up, the first thing he saw was his own name. He took it to the Commanding Officer and said, "My wife thinks I am dead". He was given compassionate leave and went to Shimla to be reunited with my mother and also to meet me for the first time.

This was truly a miracle, to have a small scrap of paper survive with the particular details of my father, to be picked up by him, having been brought to him by the wind! God works in mysterious ways. He certainly answered my mother's prayers, and those of her family.

Another event from Burma shows God's wonderful care in an emergency. When Burma gained independence from the British Commonwealth in 1948, my family were given the choice to remain in Burma and lose their British nationality or to leave the country. My family chose to do the latter and my mother, grandmother and I emigrated to England in 1949, my grandfather having passed away at the end of 1948. My father remained to complete his contract with the Burma Oil Company (BOC). In 1950 my father had an important errand to run for his boss at the BOC at the end of the day. He had to deliver an important tax form directly to the pilot of a plane bound for England. He was driving a motorbike and had called in to a petrol station before his journey. My father was stationary behind a lorry but, unfortunately, the driver reversed, without using his mirrors, straight into my Dad and he was somersaulted off his bike. We presume the lorry driver vanished quickly away from the scene but we know that Dad was robbed and left for dead in a ditch. Later that same evening a colleague from Dad's office was driving past the accident and recognised the number plate on the bike. He stopped, saw my father in the ditch and said to the people nearby, "Why didn't you help this man?" They replied, "He is dead". On checking Dad's pulse, the colleague realised Dad was still alive and with help took him to hospital.

The head of neuro-surgery in Rangoon General had a strange way of dealing with any problems/injuries connected with the brain; this was to operate on the patients to see the effect of the problem /injury on the brain! He also spent a lot of time at the races. When a messenger told him there was a serious head injury in the Casualty Department he said he had a lot of money on the next race! Instead my father was treated by an excellent neuro-surgeon who decided to observe him for the night before any action would be taken, as he had lost a lot of blood. He did lift the broken nasal bones so Dad could breathe more easily. Dad was unconscious for one month and he gradually came round and got stronger day by day. Through his firm, the BOC, he had a private room and excellent treatment. I know a lot of these details from my father and from meeting the nurse who helped him, when she came to England many years later. My mother was given regular updates on Dad's condition in England, but she also received messages from friends, some of them very alarming. One said they didn't think he would be able to talk, another said he probably wouldn't walk and never work again!

My uncle had met Dad just before he left for the airport; he also worked for the BOC and knew about the document. He managed to find it still in Dad's pocket at the hospital, as it was no use to the robbers. My uncle then made sure it was forwarded to England.

Eventually Dad made a good recovery. He had a depressed frontal bone and a fractured olfactory nerve, so he had no sense of smell but he regained all his other faculties and came to England in 1951. He managed to get a job and worked in accounts until he retired.

The end of this incident also shows God's hand at work. Shortly after he came to England my father had two weeks convalescence with an old friend, Mrs Bower, and her family in Exeter. Just after this Mrs Bower was flying to Germany to visit her son. She got into conversation with her fellow passenger and Burma came into the conversation. He said that in 1950, he was a pilot on the route between Burma and England. He said that one day a man should have brought an important document to him, but he had met with a dreadful accident and didn't arrive. He feared that the man had died. Mrs Bower assured him the man had survived and she had recently had a holiday with the same man and he was quite well and healthy.

We thank God that He led Dad's colleague to the accident site, that the right neuro-surgeon was on duty and for the excellent care he was given. We also thank God for Dad's wonderful healing and the full life he led in England. Finally we thank God that the pilot finally knew that my father was now well. This shows how God loves and cares for us.

God has shown us His power in healing. In Ashford my parents went with a group to see John Wimber in London. At the time my Dad had Rheumatoid Arthritis in his wrists and his movement in his wrists was very limited, so that he could only open a door by putting one hand over the other to turn the knob. My mother had Thallassaemia and Glaucoma. My mother went forward for healing and Dad remained in his seat. A small group of people came to Dad and said "You need prayer for healing". They put their hands on Dad's wrists and prayed. Dad testified that he had a warm feeling in his wrists. When they returned to Ashford, Dad said he could open doors with one hand. He was healed from this lack of movement and this healing remained for the rest of his life.

My mother didn't have an instant healing of her conditions, but she was given strength to live a full life and, with regular medical treatment, amazed people with her enthusiasm for being a prayer warrior and spreading the Gospel in her unique way. The doctors could not understand that she had no symptoms of Thallassaemia when she was younger, even though she was born with it. She held a very active job as an Infant Teacher with no signs of anaemia. They thought her body compensated for it in some way until she was sixty nine and fully retired. I praise God that He uses people to be channels for His healing power.

I have had many personal experiences of God's care and help and I will describe one from my time before I lived in Ashford and then some from my time at Kennington church.

I was taken into St Peter's Hospital, Chertsey, in labour for my third child at about 2.00 pm of the 18th March 1976 and I was seen by the Senior Midwife coming in to the Midwifery unit. I was put into a labour room with a nurse in attendance. As the time wore on I became aware that this nurse was not very experienced. At 5.00am, I knew my baby was in difficulties because of the length of time I had been in labour. I began to pray to Jesus, just saying His name again and again, silently asking for help.

Suddenly the door opened and the senior midwife appeared, she could see that there was staining of the waters from the door, which is a sure sign that the baby is in distress, and I heard her say, "Why didn't you buzz for help?" The nurse did not answer, but this midwife took over from her and told me exactly what to do so that Alex was delivered very quickly, at 5.35 am on 19th March 1976.

He was, however, navy blue and lifeless and both of the staff worked on him and I watched the scene unfold as though I was at the cinema. The door opened and another face appeared "I need a paediatrician at once" said the senior midwife; she must have pressed the emergency button. All the time they were working on the baby I was saying "Jesus" again and again. All of a sudden the baby made a movement, I cannot say it was a cry but both the staff present ran with him. They had been working on him for four minutes. The staff returned and completed their work with me and they assured me that he was all right, but shocked. When they had finished with me I was allowed to sleep.

My husband came to see his new son while I was sleeping. He soon noticed that there was a score on a chart by the cot which was the number seven, the other cots had a score of ten so he asked a nurse about this score and what it meant. She summoned a doctor who explained that because of the lack of oxygen at birth, Alex's condition was not bad but it was not good, hence the score. The doctor would not commit himself to what that would mean for Alex. When I found out, I knew it could mean very serious disabilities for him.

The senior midwife came to see me in the afternoon; she explained to me what had happened. Alex had been in distress for some time and the staining of the waters should have been acted on, and help sought. She told me she saw me being admitted. Then during her break on night duty, she said suddenly my name came into her mind, and she asked what did I have, a boy or girl? The other staff said I had not had the baby, so she made it her business to find out how I was. She also said she did not know why she thought of me. I said I was praying because I knew the baby needed help and she came and saved Alex. I have since been told that I could not have prayed a more powerful prayer than 'Jesus'. I knew He heard and sent the right person to help the baby. The nurse dealing with me was an inexperienced agency nurse.

This experience shows me that God is everywhere and that means I am never alone. What a comfort! He acts swiftly when we pray for help. Alex needed a lot of stimulation and care but he soon caught up with his milestones and now he excels in running marathons, with music and computers among his other talents. Thank God for His mercy.

There is another experience I can recount which is also an example of God's answer to prayer. A few years after we moved to Ashford I was working part-time as a staff nurse in a Geriatric hospital and thought my life was planned, i.e. gradually to increase my hours, go for promotion etc. This all changed when I had acute back problems with three slipped discs so I couldn't work for four years.

We had the usual problems with a growing family, stretched finances and an old car that used money as though there were no limits! I needed to return to work. One day another bill arrived for work done on the car. I prayed to God 'that if there was a job anywhere that I could do, would He lead me to it'.

The next day when I dropped Alex at school, someone suggested that I try to get a job in the schools meals service. Apparently there was a lady who worked occasionally for them and she would be there that afternoon. I returned home and began my housework. I was suddenly aware that someone said, "Phone now". It was a voice in my head. I reasoned with myself that I would wait and see the lady, who was already working for the school meals service, that afternoon. Again I heard the voice in my head, "Phone now" and again I hesitated. For the third time I was prompted, "Phone now". I stopped my work, picked up the phone book, dialled County Hall, Maidstone and asked for the number of the Ashford School Meals service. A very helpful operator put me straight through and then a lady answered and after a brief conversation told me to come and see her the next day.

The interview began with the lady telling me she was the Head of the Schools Meals Service in Ashford and she was usually out at the time my phone call came the previous day, but she had an important letter to write. Normally I would have spoken to her secretary who would have added my name to a list of people to cover for staff sickness. The interview was quite straight forward and I answered correctly that I had previous back trouble. She repeated that there was no actual job on offer but I may be called for, if her staff were off sick. However the lady appeared to change her mind and made a phone call in another room. She returned to say that I was to start work the next day at the Girls' Grammar School as they had someone off sick. I was pleased and surprised. I worked for a few days and when I knew that the member of staff was returning to work on the next Monday, I took my uniform to the cook and thanked her for the job. She said, "Hasn't anyone told you? I can keep you as our extra help."

I worked at this job for five months and then returned to nursing. In thinking back, it was a miracle that the right people were in place for my phone call, even to the Head of the service being there to speak to me personally. I was obedient to God's promptings for if I had delayed, the Head of the service would have left the office! After I prayed that prayer I had a wage every week until I retired! What an awesome God He is! It was quite embarrassing when eventually I met the lady at school who had information about the School Meals Service, to tell her I already had a job!

There are two further experiences which stand out showing God's supernatural power.

One very wet November night, I was returning home from college in my car on the M20, when I had a blowout of my nearside front tyre. I managed to get to the nearest phone on the hard shoulder. The phone was dead and I could have gone back to my car or remained by the phone. I chose to do the latter but in all the pouring rain I said the 23rd Psalm out loud. In a short while I saw a lorry drive on to the hard shoulder a short distance from my car. On the lorry was the name 'Motorway Maintenance'. A man got out wearing overalls and came towards the phone. I was just going to tell him the phone was out of order when he said to me, "You need help". He told me to stay in safety away from the traffic. Then he quickly changed the tyre using my spare tyre. I asked him how much I owed him but he said, "Nothing, just drive home and get yourself dry." He said he would follow me to make sure I was all right. I saw the man in my mirror a few times and then when I looked again there was no one behind me and there were no exits along that particular stretch of the road. I am convinced that I was sent an angel to help me. It reinforced my belief that God cares for me!

The other event happened in 2008. It was early in the morning at College. I had come to photocopy some material for the first lesson. I was on my own in the building. I was hurrying down a flight of stairs and tripped three steps before the bottom. I expected to fall heavily on my knees with a thud and to jar my entire spine. Instead I fell in slow motion and felt hands gently lift and put me down on the floor. I was completely unharmed and carried on with my work. I can only explain this by angels/or one angel lifting me up and placing me down on to the floor.

In writing about my family's experiences and my experiences I feel very grateful to have had God's love and care surround us all our lives. I have a heart full of love and praise for Him.

Stewart and Gwen French

My faith journey has had the highs and lows, peaks and troughs familiar to most believers, encompassing boarding school, where I drifted away from any faith, through college where Gwen (then my girlfriend who is now my wife), joined with others to pray for their boyfriends, and a commitment before marriage. This commitment was tested in our time in London during a three month period away from my family due to work, so when we moved to Chippenham for a new job in 1978 I only attended church to accompany Gwen 'so our children could grow up in the faith I once had.' At that point we then had been blessed with two children, Sheryl and Neil, but now have three, with the later addition of Hazel to our family after our move to Ashford.

My reawakening came in Chippenham in 1981 when Gwen and I were part of "Bind Us Together, The Musical" in which I played the part of the father in "The Prodigal Son". When Gwen and the children joined me, as we moved as a family to Kennington in 1983, the first service contained a sketch and sermon on "The Prodigal Son" – which we took as confirmation that this church is where we should worship.

Whilst we were living in Chippenham I was out of work for twelve months, during which time an offer was made for me to go to a monastery for a few days to "listen to God". I rather abruptly refused this offer, but eventually I said to Gwen, "If anybody who is not in on this suggestion says anything about it by Sunday evening, then I'll go." On that Sunday morning in church, the preacher opened her Bible and said, "The theme for today is that Jesus went away by Himself to listen to God". I went, and God spoke! There was one time when I was in a little chapel with just me, a wooden cross, a stone floor and two chairs, and I felt love pouring out of the cross to me in a way that I had never felt previously, and my tears simply flowed.

I was out of work at that time because I had been a Production Manager, a job for which I was temperamentally unsuited, and the far sighted Factory Manager took me out before I suffered physical or nervous damage – but throughout that whole time he treated me, and my family, with the utmost courtesy and respect. I was sent to a consultant to help me find work, and the 'professional' told me that at interviews I should say that I chose to leave my previous job to enable me to find a role in the area for which I was best suited – in other words, to lie. I followed his advice for over eleven months, during which time I wrote over five hundred letters (in the days before home computers!) and had over thirty interviews, to no avail. One night in bed I 'heard' God tell me that I did not trust Him, and that I should tell the truth in future – I did not know that Gwen had reached rock-bottom at that point and was praying beside me, asking what we were doing wrong! At the interview the following day I told the interviewer why I left, and he said, "I don't want a Production Manager, I want a Quality Control Manager, when can you start?" I started the job on the 9th of March 1983, moving to Ashford and finding the church family in Kennington.

In 1984 there was a lady working for me, whose mother had been diagnosed with progressive deterioration of the backbone, and was told she would never walk again unaided. I knew that I should offer to pray for her but kept on avoiding the issue. One evening I was at a men's prayer meeting at the home of Richard and Frances Eason, along with Alex and Angel (two men from Zambia): there may have been others present I am not sure. During that evening I was literally pinned to my seat – unlike in the old advert for the National Lottery with the finger coming through the ceiling and saying, "This could be YOU", I was being told, "This MUST be you", so I agreed to go on the proviso I could take someone with me. Richard Burgess, who was one of our Elders, agreed, and the date was fixed – my hope was that Richard would take the lead in the proceedings.

When we arrived at the house in Headcorn, the lady was lying on the settee. We spent around half an hour talking, when the lady asked, "Haven't you come to pray for me?" I replied, "Yes, but it probably won't be an 'Arise, get up off your bed and walk` scenario", only for her to ask, "Why, have you not got the faith for that?" - and she was a non-believer. We prayed, I laid hands gently on her - not with any great faith - but as we went to leave, she stood up from the settee and came to her front door to see us out. When Gwen and I went back to Headcorn a few months later to preach at the local Methodist Church, this lady walked one and a half miles each way with us.

Some years later we met with an American preacher who taught us about our authority as Christians. Gwen had recently returned to teaching in a small private school and had been offered, but had not yet accepted, a post in another school. She noticed a lump in her abdomen, and when she went to the Doctor she was physically examined and the lump confirmed, at which point she was told, "Don't worry, Mrs French, you will be OK after the operation" – i.e. basically, – "We'll do a hysterectomy then everything will be fine." This put Gwen in a dilemma – she wanted the new post, but could not ethically take it knowing she would be going to have a few months off sick in the near future. An appointment was made for her to have a scan at the hospital as a matter of some urgency. That evening we set to, and took authority over the spirit of cancer (Gwen's father having died of cancer this seemed a good place to start): Gwen's eyes, normally so lively and full of fun, became cold and – I think the best analogy I can come up with is 'snake-like'- as she was flung at me with her fingers reaching to scratch my eyes. Once more I rebuked whatever was in her, the sickness was cast out, and she recovered her normal composure. When she had the scan, and went back to the Doctor she was told, "We are sorry to have worried you, Mrs French, there is nothing there."

The teenage daughter of a friend of ours had been suffering severely with headaches and nausea for some days, and we were asked if we could run her up to the local hospital one evening, which we did. After an examination she was told to go home and take a couple of aspirins – whereas in the car she had told her mother that it was only the presence of her mother and boyfriend that had stopped her drifting off into unconsciousness because of the pain. The next day we received a call to ask if they could come over to our home as the daughter wanted someone to pray with her, so we collected the mother, daughter and her brother. As this family belonged to another church we went to an Elder of that church to ask if she would come and pray for healing, but in that church at the time it was only the minister who was authorised to do this praying. Whilst we did not wish to go behind the minister's back, the situation was deteriorating. When we had sent our children, and the son, off to a Youth Group for the evening, we tried to contact Frances and Richard Eason, but they were not in, nor were another couple we tried to reach. As the daughter was in extreme pain, we approached her (with her mother's blessing) to anoint her with oil for healing. She screamed and started to react in a very adverse way, so that we were concerned that there may be a death on our premises: we took authority and asked God to make her still – she calmed down immediately. When she was calm we phoned Richard and Frances again – they had just come back – and they put us on to other friends who, when we rang them, had also just come in from being out for the afternoon. The wife of that couple came round immediately, cast out the spirit of witchcraft, and the girl was able to get up – fully healed – and eat. She then went to the Youth Group but when she tried to tell them what God had done for her, nobody would believe her despite the evidence in front of their eyes. As the song says: "There are none so blind as those that will not see."

During my childhood I suffered from spasmodic jerking of the limbs, and had been diagnosed with epilepsy, meaning I had to tell the Driving Licence Centre every three years about my health, via a doctor's certificate. Any recurrence could have meant the loss of my driving licence. I had not had a company car for more than a few years when it was time for my review. During the afternoon before my appointment I had a slight recurrence of 'the jerks', but I could not face the prospect of losing the car and – possibly – also my job, so told the doctor all was well. Wives can be very perceptive, and Gwen knew instantly I walked in the door that something was up and when I told her she called a prayer meeting that evening for the church and associated friends.

Our Minister (Ted Bishop) came along to that meeting, and his wife just 'happened' to work at the surgery and be on duty the next morning, and fixed me up with an appointment with my doctor, so I could confess to him and accept whatever was coming. He asked when I was last assessed, and when I said it was over thirty years previously he made me promise not to drive until I was reassessed. In the time between my appointment with the doctor, and the one with the consultant, much happened in terms of my emotional healing, for which I will always be grateful.

When, after a couple of weeks, we went to see the consultant he looked at my notes to see who had diagnosed me in the first place – it turned out that it was the expert under whom he had studied at university. He said, "Dr X was a brilliant doctor but occasionally made some errors – let me have a look at you". After examining me from top to toe he said, "You have not got epilepsy, you have myoclonus (where the electrical impulses 'misfire' in the muscles as opposed to epilepsy when the misfiring occurs in the brain), and if you had been correctly diagnosed in the first place then the Driving Licence Centre need never have been informed."

The Full Gospel Business Men's Fellowship (FGB) has also played a large part in my experience: having had a bad experience at one of their dinners when in Wales on business I swore never to go to another meeting, but was persuaded to go to a dinner in Ashford. In the weeks prior to the dinner Gwen and I had been considering leaving the Kennington Church for reasons that are not relevant here, and on the day before the dinner we woke at about six o'clock (on a Sunday!!). We had a prayer time in the kitchen, when we were led to the analogy Jesus used of the speck of dust in your brother's eye, and piece of wood in your own. After the service we told our Elders that we were leaving, and one of them said, "If God is telling you to, then go with our blessing, if not then we'll see you back here next Sunday." At the dinner the speaker said, "We do not quote from the Bible at Full Gospel dinners, but I feel it is right to read this", and read exactly what we had been led to the day before. He also said, "I have been in Ashford for only two hours, and can see that not only is there division between churches, but division within the churches, and God is not impressed with that." After he finished speaking there was an opportunity for prayer, but so many went forward that the then President of the Ashford Chapter prayed with me, and told me what he thought God was saying. As he knew me well I was not prepared to take it from him, and basically sat and sulked. Another member of the FGB who had never met me before then offered to pray with me, and came out with exactly what the President had said, which is that we should remain in the fellowship that had nurtured us. We had been instructed, so Gwen and I stayed at Kennington.

On another occasion I had serious issues with a lady in the church, so much so that I could not even talk about her without getting angry; it was probably all my fault, but that does not matter in this context. Together with three other members of the Ashford FGB Chapter I drove up to Scotland for a Men's Weekend. During this weekend I went forward for prayer, and was laid out (slain in the Spirit) – something I had always dismissed as 'emotional reactions' or 'play acting' – but not when it happened to me. As I woke up, the lady's name was the first thing on my lips, and on the following Monday she and I ministered together at a Full Gospel dinner, and there have been no issues since (for some twenty years) – physical and emotional healings do take place.

At one time we held a Bible Study group in our home, and two ladies reported they had been diagnosed with high blood pressure. Collectively we prayed and laid hands on them. When they returned to their doctors for further checks, both reported the blood pressure was now within the normal range.

In conclusion, this is not to say that life is perfect – far from it, we still have heartaches and problems, but we know to whom we can turn in these times when we need reassurance, comfort or strength. As for God's power, His love and His care, much more has happened to us, and we have seen much more at Kennington than there is time to relate here. One example concerns a lady who had tunnel vision after an accident who was prayed for by a South African pastor and the next morning could see movement out of the side of her eyes, and now sees normally. There was also the gentleman who came to see if Kennington was where he should worship: he received his answer when the arm that was in pain before the service was healed even though nobody prayed for it specifically. There have been many other examples, but I'll leave it to others to fill in some of the gaps.

Maureen Burnham

Like so many of my generation I was sent to Sunday School, although neither of my parents attended church. My father was a convinced atheist, believing that the discoveries of Darwin made belief in the Bible impossible. My mother had room for the possibility that God existed, but kept quiet on the matter, for the sake of peace in the house. I went to Sunday School at the local Methodist chapel, and graduated to the Youth Club, which was lively and sociably minded. Faith began to seem irrelevant in my teens, the personal tragedy of my father's death further alienated me, and my twenties took me into experiences that were a world away from the church I knew. It was not until my early thirties that I began to explore this area again.

"God," I said, "I would like to believe that You exist, but I need something to convince me, not just the product of my imagination, or some overheated spiritual atmosphere. I need some proof that will satisfy my mind."

Occasionally I dropped into a service in the little Methodist chapel at Charing, right by where we were living at the time, and one evening the Bank Street Choir gave a recital there. I had always enjoyed choral singing, and, as we were shortly to move to Ashford, I enquired whether they might welcome a new member in their choir. They were indeed warmly welcoming, and I began to attend services there once we had moved. Our family commitments were increasing however. My first husband, Arthur, was working at a children's home at the time, and was increasingly drawn to the idea of fostering one of the boys. We had not, sadly, been able to have children of our own, and we could see a real need here.

I found it more and more difficult to balance the needs of a working life, the care of a child and home, and Sunday commitments. I enjoyed the singing but found no real personal incentive to faith. So I drifted away from the church to what seemed like more urgent realities.

During a stewardship campaign I was persuaded to try again. My unlikely angel was a formidable lady named Bertha, to whom it was very difficult to say no. I resumed choir practice and services, intending to stay for a short while and then quietly fade out again. This was where God had other ideas. We were practising *Messiah* one Thursday evening at choir practice, and the men were in serious difficulties with the chorus, *"All we like sheep"*. One particularly strong tenor was indeed leading the rest of the tenors astray. In the end the exasperated choirmaster stopped us. "Ladies," he said, "take a rest while I work with the men on this." I sat back and looked down the church to the window, where pigeons were wheeling outside in the late spring evening. Unexpectedly I was enfolded in the love of God. It was like nothing I had ever dreamed of, read of, or believed possible. I was aware that I was held in the Father's love. I knew that I was loved, that God knew everything about me, including bits I would not want even my nearest and dearest to know. I was comprehensively known, accepted, and comprehensively loved. My own love flowed back to Him. If someone loves you so deeply for who you are, warts and all, how can you not love them back? Later I came across the scripture, "We love because He first loved us," and I thought, Yes, that's exactly how it is.

I don't know how long it lasted, probably only a few seconds, but it was a life changing experience. God had met with me, not in an emotional setting, but in a way that totally satisfied my request. I attached myself strongly to the life of the church, and began to make some firm friendships. I felt so joyful. Arthur noticed the difference and began to talk of coming to church himself. Then the clouds began to gather. Arthur was a diabetic, and gashed his leg while doing some woodwork. The wound would not heal and the circulation in his leg was affected. The doctor referred him to hospital, where they talked of the dangers of gangrene and an amputation. A friend suggested that we attend a healing service at Tunbridge Wells, one of a series where some remarkable healings had been witnessed. In desperation Arthur agreed. At the service he went forward in response to a call to make a commitment to Christ and was ushered away by a helper. He missed the main healing focus when the visiting evangelist prayed for those needing healing. I squirmed desperately in my seat. We had come for healing and I thought we were in danger of missing it. After the service I met him in the hall. He was radiant and dismissed my fears. "It's OK," he said. "After praying about my response to Christ, he prayed over my leg. I can feel circulation coming back. In fact it's jolly painful. Don't be alarmed if I yell on the way back." He did, alternating cries of pain with cries of thanks to God.

At this time our URC minister, Richard Davis, was seriously exercised about the future of Kennington Church. He suggested to a group of us that we dedicate a weekend of prayer and praise to waiting on the Lord. We would particularly pray to discern the way forward for this small and struggling church. One of our number was Phyllis Hull, a faithful pillar of that church. Phyllis broke down in tears over the current situation, and we committed ourselves as a group to pray and help in whatever way we might.

Richard was considering the shape of his ministry in Ashford, and subsequently decided to withdraw from any substantial input in Bank Street Church Sunday mornings, taking services instead at both Cade Road and Kennington churches, travelling from one to the other, and thereby ensuring his consistent presence and encouragement to the two congregations. I began to attend evening services at Kennington, which encouraged me to pray a little more knowledgeably for that church.

Meanwhile our own personal storm clouds deepened and darkened. Arthur suffered a stroke, and was taken to the Brook Hospital in London. The prognosis was not good. The consultant told me that it was probably the result of a small clot in the bloodstream, due to soft veins damaged by his diabetes. The clot, or flake, was too small to be precisely identified at that time, and was likely to circulate round his system, causing more strokes and ultimately a fatal one. I could not and did not believe that this was God's will for us. I asked a group of friends to pray with Arthur, convinced that God would answer our prayers. As we did, Arthur's hand, curved over as a result of the stroke, straightened and became usable again, though it never regained its former flexibility. More importantly, there was no recurrence of the stroke. We could believe that the clot had been dispersed.

However one thing followed another. It was found that Arthur's kidneys were now failing. This time there was no assurance of a full healing and we had no urge to pray in the former way. He was a very sick man, and his immune system was failing. The consultant predicted a few months left, but Arthur survived a year. He saw another spring and rejoiced in the beauty of the cherry tree flowering outside his window, but the relentless strain was taking its toll of both of us. When he caught a cold, a serious business for a man in his condition, he told me that he would contrive to get himself transferred to hospital. The doctor was reluctant to send him, Arthur was found on the floor, having fallen out of bed when nobody was in the room and was duly sent to hospital. Once there, he stopped struggling to live and passed peacefully away. It was just before Easter.

We held a funeral service at Bank Street Church, followed by a short service at Charing crematorium. I don't know quite what I was expecting, perhaps some sense of blessing at the main service. What happened was quite extraordinary, and it happened at the crematorium. As we concluded the service with the hymn *The Lord's my Shepherd*, I heard some extraordinary and quite unearthly harmonies. I thought I was dreaming or fantasising in what I knew was a highly emotional state, but outside two other people asked me whether I had heard the wonderful singing. We realised that we had heard the angels sing. I have never heard it since, though I live in hope that one day I may. Why for Arthur? I believe it may have been because at the end he sacrificed himself and the life he had left, however little, for me. Arthur was a lover of life and a fighter. He did not want to die, but he believed it was the best thing he could offer me. Jesus said, "Greater love hath no man than this, that he lay down his life for his friends." I believe it was this sacrificial love that was celebrated at Arthur's funeral service, and it humbles me.

In the next few years the fellowship at Kennington church grew. Some came to a more active and dynamic faith. Others were drawn in by family and friends and made their own commitment. Some joined us on moving into the area. Each had their own story of an encounter with grace. New housegroups were organised, as well as prayer twins and triplets. A number of baptisms took place. There was a vibrancy in the air, a sense of expectation that God would act in dynamic ways. Worship took on a new dimension, preaching, particularly that of our minister, became words that spoke to the heart. Two Elders were appointed to oversee the daily life of the church and to ensure some continuity when Richard Davis left in the mid eighties for another ministerial post. During this time my health and energy was declining, and I needed a major operation. The prayerful love and support that surrounded me at that time was a personal revelation of the church as family, and encouraged me to commit myself fully to worship at Kennington.

The subsequent departure of a large number of members after the appointment of a new minister appeared to be a major blow to the church. Those of us remaining had to rebuild and refill major church offices that were now left vacant. We were helped by a word from Paul Burnham, coming to preach the Sunday following the exodus, "Fear not, little flock, for it is your Father's good pleasure to give you the kingdom." We received it as a personal word of encouragement. We drew closer together and our family feeling increased. I became an Elder, together with Jill Pearson and a little later, Joe Kavanagh, under the encouragement of Ted Bishop, our Methodist minister, who helped to guide us through the first difficult years. We became convinced, as time went on, that we were called as a church to become a kind of hospital to care for those in need, to pray for their healing and restoration, and sometimes their moving on to serve Christ in different spheres.

Once again there were some remarkable stories of people touched by God's grace and moving into ministry or mission work. We had established contacts with American Christian leaders, some of whom began to visit us on a regular basis, helping to strengthen and widen our faith. Our church strove to be, in its own particular way, a place where God's love was expressed in action. Those called to be pillars of the church were bonded together; it is a bond that still holds strong, even for those who no longer worship regularly at the church.

I was able to take an early retirement from my work and explore a call to preach. I had understood God to be asking me to consider this for some time, and that now the time had arrived. I trained under URC auspices, and have since preached and taken services in URC, Methodist and Anglican churches as part of my service for God. When I first realised that God was pointing me in this direction, I asked Him, "Why me, what had I got to say that was special?" The answer formed in my mind in the words of a song I had heard. "Tell My people I love them, tell My people that I care. When they feel far away from Me, tell My people I am there."

In 1996 Paul Burnham and I were married at Bank Street Church (now Centrepiece) and held our wedding reception at Kennington church. It was a very happy time. Paul and Wendy had joined the Kennington church in order to candidate jointly for the URC ministry, but Wendy's sickness and subsequent death had made this impossible. Paul had been through hard times after the death of his first wife Wendy, and our growing closeness flowered into the possibility for something more. Although we ceased after marriage to worship regularly at Kennington, committing ourselves to local worship at Wye, we have kept contact through taking occasional services, and through the strong bonds of friendship that we made there. It's a particular pleasure that Paul's son Hugh and his wife Jane began to worship there shortly before we left. The family connection continues.

We divide our time in Wye, when not out on the circuit preaching, between the lively Anglican church and the small

Methodist congregation. We have initiated a tea service at the latter, which takes the form of a tea around the table for half an hour, a talk or presentation by a speaker, taking the place of a sermon in a main service, and a short service of hymn and prayer to conclude. We find that there is indeed strength and blessing in the diversity of a large church, but there is also blessing in the closeness of a small number of people gathered for worship and fellowship. I count myself blessed in this latter part of my life, in the new family that I have been given through Paul, and the strength of Christian fellowship I have found in Wye.

May Collins

This is a transcript of an address by the late May Collins given at Kennington United Reformed Church on 12th July 1998 in which she recounted some of her experiences of Missionary work in Tamil Nadu, India.

Revival in the Church in South East India

<u>The Story of the Boy with the Fish – the Children's Talk</u>

They are often hungry in India, and they don't have very much money. There was a little boy called Yayserdasen, who was told by his mother to go to the market and buy a few vegetables. So he took the basket, not the sort of basket that we have, but a round basket that you carry on your head – that's the way they carried baskets in India.

And so he went off. He hadn't got much money, but he got the things that his mother wanted, and put them in the basket, and he started off home.

He had to walk about a mile to get home; it was rather hot and he was getting a bit tired. As he looked around he saw that there was a gap in the hedge. It was a prickly hedge, and he looked through and there was a trickle of water, coming down, under the hedge and out into the road. Now that was very unusual, because there isn't very much water around in streams and ponds, so he thought, "Where does that come from, I've never seen that before". So he banged the bushes down with a stick and got through the hedge and there was a big muddy pool of water in front of him. Again he said, "Well, I've never seen this before."

He then noticed there was another channel of water joining the pool, and then he looked at the pool and it was all muddy, but he saw there was something wriggling in it. He thought "That must be a fish, I wonder if I could catch it?"

So he stepped out into the water: he didn't wear shoes on his feet, and he felt about in the water until he felt that something wriggling – the tail of the fish – and he thought, "I'm not going to let this go!" so he pulled and pulled, and out came the fish.

He thought, "We haven't had fish curry for a long time!" When the fish stopped wriggling, he put it in the basket and got back though the prickly hedge, put the basket on his head and set off for home.

As he walked back the head of the fish was sticking out of the basket on one side, and the tail of the fish was sticking out on the other side, and people who were coming the other way offered him money for the fish. One said, "I'll give you a rupee for that fish", and another said, "I'll give you two rupees", but he said, "No! I'm taking it home."

When he had nearly got home, he thought of something; it was just as if somebody spoke to him: "There are people at a meeting over in the village of Alambadi, and they haven't got anything to eat. You take the fish to them, and then you can all share it together for a picnic." He pondered for a minute and he thought, "Maybe my mother is over there, I'll go and see."

So he went to the village and they were singing Tamil lyrics, just like we sing our songs to Jesus. He saw his mother looking at him, and he went over and said to her, "Look, I've got this fish!". His mother replied, "We have just been praying that the Lord will give us something to eat before we all go home." They had all brought some rice and some grain, and they were already cooking it. The boy said "I've got the fish and I believe that Jesus has given it to me. Here it is." So when they had finished the service, they cooked the fish. They had to wait a little while, but they made a lovely fish curry together.

This shows us that if we ask the Lord, if we really need something, He helps us and He gives it to us.

The Coming of the Mettur Dam

I want to speak about Revival this morning. Revival means simply 'Seeing Jesus together', and if you think about John Wesley, he went up and down Britain, preaching the Gospel, with the anointing of the Spirit sometime ago now, (I'm not very good at dates). Many of you have read about John Wesley in his journals. When he preached the Gospel, something happened – the people repented, they came to see the Lord, and there was a great time of joy and gladness. Out of that time of blessing came the Methodist Church.

When there is a time of revival, it means that people, somehow, have been given by the Lord, 'seasons of rejoicing', which is what Peter the Apostle spoke of: seasons of rejoicing in the presence of the Lord. When that happens, there is a liberation of the Holy Spirit. For those who don't know the Lord, it is as if they are magnetised and drawn into where Christians are praising the Lord.

We read that beautiful passage from Isaiah 35 v 1 together this morning, "The desert shall rejoice and blossom as the rose, the wilderness shall be glad, the blind shall see, the ears of the deaf shall be unstopped, and the lame shall leap for joy" – all of that applies very much to me! But when it happens, it says, "The desert shall rejoice and blossom as the rose, there's going to be a way of holiness opened up. Sorrow and sighing shall flee away, and gladness and joy will come into lives that are having problems." That's what the Lord did for that village that I was telling the children about – Alambadi – it was a desert place.

Very few of you will have lived in a desert or even camped in a desert, a place where there is very little rain, everything is dry and barren, no birds sing, and the people are sad and depressed. In that village they were very poor indeed, but something happened. About six or seven miles away, British engineers had built a big dam, which was finished in the 1940's.

They built this big dam between two mountains, and when I arrived in India this was one of the first things that they took me to see. It was a mile to walk across it, and slowly the waters gathered up behind it, with Alambadi about six miles away as the crow flies. After the dam had been there a year or two they decided to cut a canal, for all those stricken villages, down to join another river bed. So all the villagers were hired, they were paid very meagre wages, but for once they worked with a will, and all the way up that line they cut the channel to reach the dam.

Eventually it was finished and then the great day came and all along the line the villagers gathered and waited. When they opened the sluice gates at Mettur Dam the water just poured out. There was already an electric generating station there, the water poured out of the sluice gates and it roared down the canal. It came with a mighty rush; there was a terrific force of water that had built up in front of the dam, and they heard it coming before they saw it. When they saw it, as you can imagine, everybody jumped for joy. They rejoiced, they flung themselves about, they were so happy. The children had to be stopped from falling into it. And so the water rushed through and joined the river some distance away, and to about seven or eight villages, that meant a lifeline. If you went back four months later, you would see it, as we did see it. I didn't see the waters come down, (that was just one occasion), but I saw the rice fields and the grain growing as fresh crops on each side of the canal, all the way down the length of the canal.

Now in that village, there was a teacher, not very highly qualified, called Poniah, who went to one of our mission rallies in a place called Erode. That was also not a very big place, but the word of God was preached there with power, and with authority.

41

Poniah was the only one there from his village, but he went back to that village a transformed man. He was the only teacher in the village school, his wife was illiterate; in fact most of the grown-ups in the village were illiterate. But he brought the word of God, first of all to the children, they had a picture of the Good Shepherd. Poniah soon became quite well known all around, and the Hindu people came with their problems and he was able to help them. A great blessing fell upon that village, and the Word of God grew. And so it was that when the river watered the land, God watered the people with the Living Word in Alambadi.

<u>Salem</u>

Salem is a big town of about three hundred thousand people, a collection of villages. In the centre of that town there is a big area of land, that, way back in the 1850's, was given by the government to the London Missionary Society, to develop a High School, which they built. It was opened about 1860, becoming very well known in the town, and they built a church at one corner. I suppose that the land in the middle of the town was about eight acres. So there were playing fields for the High School, a house for the Christian Pastor, and in the corner of the compound they built a church.

The way opened for an Indian Evangelist, who was called the "John Wesley of South India" to come and speak to the group. Meetings were arranged and within about two weeks about three hundred people gathered together. We moved out all the benches (we didn't have seats, we had benches) and everybody sat on the floor, and so we got about three to four hundred people, crowded together, men on one side, women on the other, and Brother Daniel and his team of speakers conducted a Mission. I think they were there for about four days. They took the opening theme: 2 Chronicles Chapter 7 and verse 14. He was Telugu, but preached in English. He didn't speak Tamil, but he had a Tamil interpreter in his team, so the message was given in two languages, and they preached from 2 Chronicles 7:14 for two solid days morning and evening: "If My people who are called by My name will humble themselves and pray, and seek My face, and will turn from their wicked ways. then I will hear from Heaven, will forgive their sin and will heal their land".

He and the other members of his team preached about sin and the results of sin. There was singing, but the cement got very hard after about two hours. Food was provided in the school, which was on holiday, but Daniel's team was staying with us, in our house. I said to Brother Daniel, rather in despair, at the end of the second night, "How much longer before we hear the word of salvation? I know we don't understand, but when are we going to hear about the love of God breaking through." He said, "You do not know my people. It's coming. You sit down and wait patiently."

So we went back the next day, and then his wife spoke, and she spoke rather differently, she spoke about how the Lord provided the food that they needed, they lived from one day to the next. And then it changed and he spoke about the cross and the meaning of the cross.

At the end of the middle of the fourth day he said, "Now, we're going to sing, and then I want some people to pray, as the Lord leads you. And if you want to pray there is no need for one only to pray, the Lord can hear if two or three pray at once. Pray as you feel led by the Holy Spirit." And we all knelt down to pray – still on the hard cement! There were a few elderly men there sitting on the benches. Not the women, the women didn't sit on the benches, they sat on the floor.

We started to pray and something happened. It's very difficult to explain what happened, but the people there were burdened with many family problems. There was unhappiness in the family and in the church, there were rivalries in the High School. The preaching had been given in the power of the Spirit, and the people began to pray, first one and then another, and then there was a murmur of prayer going up all over the building. Some of them were weeping, and there was a good deal of noise and commotion. The noise grew louder and louder, and I noticed several people whom I knew, coming in from the villages, sitting down and joining the crowd. I wondered ..... because I thought, "I have never seen anything like this before.." Was it mass hysteria, or was something really happening? I didn't know, I couldn't tell, I was too bewildered.

It went on and at last they dispersed. They had the benediction and some of them went home: others didn't go and stayed all night, but we went home. The next day we saw what was going to happen. Very soon after this Brother Daniel left, but that wasn't the end ... that was only the beginning.

The first thing which happened was people began to give back things that didn't belong to them. Chairs and tables came back into the school. All sorts of things came back into our bungalow – Christmas decorations that I had put up, little things. But more than that people began to be reconciled. I saw two women in the time of prayer, get up from where they were sitting and come and kneel down. I knew those women, they had not been on speaking-terms for years. I saw them weeping together and I thought, "This is the Lord, praise God, this is the Lord, this is the Kingdom!"

Good News

Good News has got a marvellous way of spreading. I know bad news spreads, but good news spreads too. The youth of the church, young students, boys and girls, sat in different groups, but they met together in a meeting. They had a youth meeting in our bungalow. That was after the church services when the blessing was beginning to grow and spread to other places.

I was out visiting a neighbour and I was coming back down the drive, they were all there and they were all singing. They were singing a lyric; they were singing in such a way I stopped to listen. I was outside and it was just like the incense altar that we read about in the Tabernacle. The prayer was in the singing. There was a note, I am not exaggerating, there was a note in the singing which was above their human voices, and it was just as if the angels were joining in. I was right outside the building and I could hear it. I could see the offering being lifted up to the Lord in praise and worship.

We had a time of prayer and testimony and the people who had come had all been blessed greatly, all the young people. They'd all got a new vision; they all wanted to say something. More or less they all listened to one another before they started, and then we had some kind of refreshments. There were a lot of them there and we had a job to find enough cups or tumblers and plates to go round, to give them coffee and biscuits. When we were handing it round, they were all sitting on the floor, and I remember my best crockery service, that I had kept for years without it being used, all spread all over the floor. I looked at it and thought, "Well most of this will get broken, but it doesn't matter two hoots now, this is the Kingdom – everything is changing, everything is different. The Lord is here, Jesus is here". Strangely enough, not a single cup was broken! It wouldn't have mattered a bit if it had been, it is just as if the Lord smiled and all the cups were there!

And there were so many other things that happened.

Mutasami

There was one man who went back to his village; his name was Mutasami. He was completely illiterate; he was a leader, and he always led in the wrong way. There was a certain amount of land which had been given for his tribe of people, (they were rather a low-caste tribe). They were allotted land, and the government gave the Christian section of that group to the Missionary Society to look after, and to develop a fellowship, a community, villages along that stretch of land. So there was often friction from the villagers who didn't think that they were getting all the things that they could have received from the Mission.

I can remember that man, coming with a group of protesters, when a committee meeting was being held in our house, circling the house, shouting at the top of his voice his complaints and grievances against the society, because they hadn't got all the things they wanted. And I remarked to one person, "It would take the Archangel Gabriel to convert that man!".

I saw that man, in his village. He was the only one in his village to visit Salem. They didn't have a church; they only had a few posts with a shelter over the top. They didn't have much money. But this man had a farm of about three acres on which he grew rice, so he was comparatively well off. When he got back to his village, he stood up and said, "I've got something to say to you. First of all I'm going to give money to three of the young men to go back to Salem and meet the people in the Lechler Church – they will tell you what happened, but I have seen the Lord Jesus." He looked at his brother, in the front row, and he said, "Yes, I know why you are looking at me, I've owed you ten rupees for the last three years, well here it is! And I want to tell the others, who I know I owe you money: I can't pay you all at once, but I promise, I will pay you – Jesus has really come into my life, and it's going to be different." And they all listened, and that evening they all went along to try and hear a bit more – what on earth had happened to Mutasami?

And things like that went on happening and the glory spread.

The Joy
And the joy ...

Thinking about it since there are so many cases of that in our history – of blessings – and of course John Wesley – the Methodist Church sprang out of blessings like that. And I thought, "What is the heritage that we have entered into out of revival?" And there were several things that just came quite simply.

First a terrific Spirit of liberation in the church: liberation and joy. Worries and tribulations, yes there will be, the Lord said so, but He would provide.

The next thing is that the Bible becomes a living book. That's what happened after the meeting in Salem, the bookshop that we ran sold out of Bibles the next day. They kept ordering fresh ones and the Bibles were sold continually, and people were reading them, and the Bible became alive, with verses of scripture being quoted here and there.

And the sick were healed. I should say that the man who had been dismissed and who was fasting on the church steps, was at the meetings and stopped fasting after William Ngenda, the Aftrican, had prayed with him. He went to the headmaster, who was the one who dismissed him, and said, "Look, I want to pray with you, I'm sorry. I believe that if we can pray together, your son will be healed." (The son was suffering from typhoid fever.) They prayed together those two men, they went and knelt down by the son. The son had a high delirious fever. I know what it's like, because I had typhoid. The next day the fever was down to normal, and it didn't come back.

There were other cases like that: of broken relationships that were healed. Husbands and wives, relations, all kinds of things. When a child was sick, any Christian would go next door to another Christian to ask "Come and pray with me, my child is sick." And so the glory went on.

Now I cannot say that the glory has lasted to this day, as there are seasons of revival, but there are times when the fire dies down. But out of the fire, out of those times, come leaders.

The Leaders

There were leaders who came out of that fire. Rama Chunda, the man who had been dismissed, wasn't given his job back in the High School, but he came up to our office, where we needed somebody. And he became a friend and he became a great blessing to us.

We always met together at ten, in the bungalow, to have coffee and refreshments; we started work at eight. He said, "I'm going to take Ministerial Training", and he did. We went to the prayer meeting before he went off to college. He was an educated man, a Brahmin of a lower caste. We went to his house. He said "You'll have to come to my house to pray, before I go."

We all went. I went with a certain amount of trepidation as his wife had just recovered from typhoid. I thought, "The infection is probably still there, and we're going to eat and drink in that house. But we can't refuse it – the Lord give us all protection." – I prayed that in silence. We all partook and he went forth with blessing, and nobody got any infection: he took his training and he was made a pastor in the Nilgiri Hills, which is another story altogether. But he went and he took the blessing with him, the blessing spread over into the

Nilgiri Hills. It also spread into that village where Mutasami repaid his debts – Zacchaeus all over again.

They built a church – we all built a church together there, and the blessing spread from place to place. So we can look forward with joy to times of refreshing. The wind of the Lord is moving in this place too. The wind of the Lord, the "Marching at the top of the trees" (described in 2 Samuel 5 v2) is going forth now. And the Lord is going forth in this country and I am sure there are the signs there for us to see that the blessing will come.

I remember that Donald (May's husband) and Joe Kavanagh tried going into one of the local pubs some years ago; they went down and had just a couple of drinks and sat down and talked to the people. Joe used to go there before, Donald had never been, but Joe took him along and Joe knew the people. After about three weeks the landlord of the pub came and said "I understand you came in with a good motive, but would you please stay away. I'd much rather that you didn't come anymore." So the door was closed. But you see it was closed because there wasn't any collective prayer behind it, although Joe and Donald prayed before they went.

We're not going to reach the public house that way. But the magnetism of the Holy Spirit is to draw people in, I don't think I shall live to see it, but I do know that this church will one day be full of people praising the Lord – you may even have to move the chairs and sit on the carpet. To God be the glory, the sound of marching is going forward in the trees, and we shall see it here in Kennington.

In other places too, Shirley knows that the wind of change is moving and people are going forward in Willesborough Baptist Church and it will be so everywhere.

I finish with a testimony that Arthur Wallis gave, he had a vision in which he was standing on the top of the church tower in Kennington, and he saw little lights burning all the way round in a circle. He asked the Lord what it meant, and He replied, "They are the fires of blessing, and they are going to spread from place to place, in every denomination all around the area." That was the prayer of Arthur Wallis. He is with the Lord, but I'm sure he knows what's happening, and he will be seeing what will happen in the days to come, and we can praise the Lord for it.

Thank you very much for listening.

Hugh Burnham

An Account of My Calling

"All my uncles are Vicars." says Sam to Chief Superintendant Foyle, when she tells him she has invited her uncle, Rev. Aubrey Stewart, to stay at Foyle's house.

Whoever said, "God has no Grandchildren" was quite right – each of us needs to form our own relationship with God the Father. To each of us He offers the chance to be His child, a son or daughter of the Most High God. The Christians of every generation are First Generation Christians.

But it does sometimes "run in the family". It ran in Jesus' family. His uncle Zechariah was a Priest, and his cousin John was a Baptist. He could trace his ancestry back to King David; two of Jesus' brothers (James and Jude) have books included in our Bible.

When His mother and brothers came looking for Him, He said, "Who is My mother and who are My brothers?" And He stretched out His hand toward His disciples and said, "Here are My mother and My brothers! For whoever does the will of My Father in heaven is My brother and sister and mother."

It is a historical fact that my great grandfather was a Methodist Local Preacher in the Maidstone (Salem) Primitive Methodist Circuit. Both my maternal and paternal grandfathers, and my mother were Methodist Local Preachers, and my father still is. It may have been an influence, but it counts for nothing in the Kingdom of Heaven.

While none of this heritage counts for anything in terms of spiritual merit, it is true that we often need someone to "take us to Jesus". My parents certainly did that – and took me to a good few Christian worship services too. A varied ecclesiastical diet, because, as a child, I sang in the Parish Church choir, as well as accompanying my parents on their preaching appointments.

Although piano lessons were not a great success, I did pick up my Nan's cheap plywood guitar, and her "Teach Yourself" book and learn to strum some chords. At that time most Methodist Services were a hymn sandwich with traditional hymns accompanied by a keyboard instrument of some kind – piano, harmonium, or organ, and Wye Methodist Church was no exception. But every now and then a visiting preacher or team would introduce us to new kinds of song, led by alternative instruments.

At that time Syd Doyle was a lay pastor in the Methodist Circuit, and he was often accompanied by his wife Liz. Liz led songs with her 12 string guitar. I looked forward to services led by them, or by groups of students from Wye College.

The Methodist Revival Fellowship held regular conferences at the Hayes Christian Conference Centre in Derbyshire – one of these had worship led by Ken McDougall and Gill Hargeaves, who were joined by a chap who played electric guitar. It is strange to think how radical this seemed at the time. Electric guitar was associated with exactly-not-the-sort-of-music which one had in church. Yet the sweet and mellow harmonies which he extracted from this "instrument of the devil" were an instant hit with the delegates.

Gill and Ken gave these revivalist meetings a soundtrack I shall never forget. I use some of the songs I learned from them to this day – though sadly the rich harmony of their voices is harder to reproduce. I remember my mother asking Gill where they found the music for their songs. And that a copy of "Songs of Fellowship" (then a slim volume of about one hundred songs) was then purchased at the earliest opportunity.

Taking part in Christian Union activities, both at Portsmouth Polytechnic, and at Wye College introduced me to other young Christians, and provided me with opportunities to lead Christian songs. I am indebted to "Bod" and his girlfriend who mentored my guitar playing and gave me an opportunity to purchase the Yamaha 12 string guitar that I cherish to this day.

In September 1986, I married Jane, and in doing so gained a soul-mate who shared a love of contemporary Christian music. We made our new home in Gravesend.

We went together to Greenbelt Festival, and Easter People. A Christian record label called "Ears and Eyes Music", was promoting its artists like Martyn Joseph and organised a series of festivals called "Impact" one of which was held at Gravesend. We were also listening to Michael Fanstone, the Baptist Minister from Gravesend, who had a regular radio show on a Local Radio station. For an hour or so each week, Christian music replaced the more normal commercial radio playlist.

In Gravesend we made new friends, not least by attending the Methodist Church in the town centre. Not only were there many young people in the church, but some families had attended Christian Festivals like "Spring Harvest", and were asking questions like, "Why can't the services in church be like Spring Harvest – they have a worship band and sing modern worship songs?" The church let me lead some songs from Songs of Fellowship before each service began. It may not have been quite "Spring Harvest" but people seemed to enjoy learning the new songs. I also took my guitar and books to the Bible studies and house groups that we attended.

There was one chap who never came to church, but was always a regular at Dr. Laity's Bible Class. I remember he drew me quietly aside, pressed a sum of money into my hand and told me to "buy some more of those orange books – you haven't got enough to go round." So I did, and felt a great encouragement from his faith in me.

It was at about this time that I began to think that in the midst of this, there was a call to lead worship. A "call" seems to me to have three elements, firstly that you see a need which is not being met, secondly a feeling (for want of a better word) that you might be the person to meet that need, and thirdly the prompting of the Spirit – through unsolicited comments and the sort of "God-incidences" that suggest, "He's trying to tell me something". I perceived a need among God's people for a more modern style of worship, particularly among the smaller chapels and churches who didn't have access to the music groups that some of the larger churches had.

There was a slight problem, however, in that the Methodist Church, at that time, did not have "Worship Leaders", it only had "Preachers". My calling was very much to lead worship. The call was strong enough for me to discuss the matter with our Minister, Rev. Roger Cresswell. He was very encouraging but emphasised that the process of becoming a Methodist Local Preacher has always been to "test the call". If at any time one realises that the call is not real, there is no shame in stopping. So, on this basis I commenced preaching and studying under the expert tutelage of Elizabeth Cresswell, Roger's wife, who was a Local Preacher and later became ordained as a Methodist Minister. Although Methodist churches, being made of people, are as diverse as people can be, there seemed to be a place for a few songs in almost every service. In places it became possible to work and play with the local musicians; I like to think I might have encouraged one or two along the way.

Although a change of job in 1988 gave me more free time, it was hard to find time and enthusiasm to write essays and read theological books. But, I did manage to pass the exams and in 1993, just before we left Gravesend and moved to Wye, I became a fully accredited Methodist Local Preacher.

Of course, in Methodism, one learns "on the job", and the five or six years I spent studying were also spent preaching. The call did not diminish. It is a privilege to lead God's people in Worship. And I learned to value the preaching part of the job also, as "the Word" is an integral part of the whole worship service.

At Kennington we have found a place where God's people are keen to worship and share in worship. And by travelling with guitar in one hand, and a Bible in the other, it seems, I can still bring something "different" to worship in the little churches around our Methodist Circuit.

Bernadette and Bob Staiano

We were associated with Kennington United Reformed/ Methodist Church during the nineteen eighties, and were particularly blessed by the depth of support and fellowship we experienced at Kennington. Bob was not a Christian when he started attending the church. Bernadette took the children to the women's group where I remember good fellowship with a good crowd of women, some from Bank Street church and others just from the neighbourhood. We did flower arranging and all sorts of crafts and activities, enjoyed fun evenings and Christmas meals together at the church.

It also became a bit of a tradition for the women to take the Mothering Sunday service and also the Christmas morning service. This gave wonderful opportunity for the women to use their talents and giftings. Bernadette remembers the Monday mothers and toddlers Bible study group where the mums sat in a circle with the children playing in the middle, while Richard Davies taught them about the love of Jesus.

It was during the time when Richard Burgess and Janet Huang (Dray) were Elders that Bob came to the Lord. At this time the church was regularly filled to capacity, with the rear sliding doors opened and every space filled. Sunday school was so well attended that Phyllis Hull's class had to be accommodated in a caravan in the car park. Our daughter (Yolande) remembers being regularly rewarded, along with others, with foreign chocolate bars for reciting the memory verse correctly – but quite often only after several other children had gone first! They loved Phyllis and she was a good sport.

The children's holiday clubs led by Alf Hart and team were a great success and drew in many local children for the week. Numbers reached a hundred or so. Different themes were used to present the gospel. One year Alf made a wooden Gospel Ship that stood at the front of the church. Another year the lounge was turned into a spaceship and the children had to wear a space helmet to go in.

We vividly remember the day when Bob was baptised along with three others. It was a blessed day, not least because of the miracle of healing experienced by one of the candidates. She had chronic pain and restricted movement in her knee, but after her baptism she could move it freely and without pain,

Roger and Sue Rigg were leading the youth work and it so grew in size that it became necessary to divide it into two groups. Roger and Sue took the younger ages in the church and we took the older children to our home. For both of us this was very much trial and error, but in faith and wanting to play our part we pressed on. Some years later one of the children, now a young adult, greeted us at a Christian event at the Stour Centre and was keen to tell us that she had recently come to the Lord and been baptised. Even more years later an adult lady serving in a coffee shop recognised us from the time she attended the youth group and was keen to talk about the happy times she had enjoyed at the group.

Although we have been led to worship in another fellowship, the bonds and friendship with Kennington are still strong, and we have been back several times to share in the morning worship, and to preach: friendships forged over many years cannot easily be broken.

Joe Anthony

I was and always have been a believer in God, I'll get that out of the way first, in case you were expecting some tale of drugs and debauchery with the attendant rock'n'roll life style.

Rock'n'roll lifestyles failed to happen in sleepy little Kent villages, where I grew up. My upbringing would have made the Famous Five jealous. Woods and hills with attendant ruined farmyards to roam and play in. Close knit, village friends that stayed friends right through secondary school and on into adulthood. A 'benign neglect' parenting style that allowed such free roaming and the time to enjoy a heaven-sent childhood.

So with nothing to rebel against and a laid back attitude verging on lazy I grew into adulthood with none of the 'interesting' personality disorders that one expects every well adjusted person to have these days.

I have no idea why I believed in God, I just did and I see no reason to analyse this any further. I did not however believe in Jesus! I knew that someone called Jesus had once existed and done great things. I studied history at school and I know all about first and secondary source material, and there is enough of that to prove He was a real person. But as for being the Son of God and the rest, well let's just say I was sceptical.

At the age of thirty I fell in love for the first time and married Jennifer as soon as I could. This sounds simple but to reach this wonderful point some even more wonderful things had to happen to me first. Kennington Church plays a pretty important part in this. To say that Jenni was involved in this church would be an understatement. She had been a Christian for many years and had the 'interesting' lifestyle that I so failed to have. So there was this church-going woman who I happened to be in love with; she asked if I was willing to go with her to church. I liked church (C of E primary school, church at Easter and Christmas), I enjoy singing hymns, the praying I could take or leave, but I'm never one to shirk my responsibilities. I left church that first Sunday with some firm impressions both on the type of church and the congregation. I will keep those to myself as I count many of those same people as friends now and my initial impressions were not good.

With hindsight it is clear that this wariness and suspicion was a blatant attack. Little did I know that in a few short months I would be a full Christian. I was still attending Kennington most weeks with Jenni, after all I was in love, and getting used to the more freeform worship that my limited C of E experience had not equipped me for. The more I attended, the more I talked to people, the more I came to respect and understand what it was to live a Christian lifestyle. I just failed to 'believe' in Jesus, so while

I was happy to attend, it always felt like a hollow attempt to ingratiate myself with Jenni and her friends. I'm sure the more astute members of the congregation had me pegged for a non-believer from the word go but still they welcomed me with open arms, sometimes a little too open for my liking.

My relationship with Jenni was beginning to hit the rather large problem of my lack of Christian faith and things were looking bleak. I began to dislike going to church and other, more worldly, things became important again. My church attendance, not surprisingly, began to slip.

A motorcycle crash is never something to rejoice in, but maybe I should! 1999 and the big solar eclipse was due. Jenni and I planned to travel down to Cornwall to my Mum's holiday cottage for a better view. It would have been a good weekend even though things had become strained between the two of us. It would have been good if we had arrived! The Motorbike, a Honda VFR750FL for those that have an interest, ploughed into a van at about sixty miles an hour. Both of us should have died! Both of us survived to the amazement of the attending paramedics. A short stay in Exeter hospital and we completed our journey down to Cornwall in a hospital car for some rest and recuperation. Things naturally had hit an all time low between Jenni and myself. She had no wish to be there; I had lost my beloved motorcycle and was looking at three months off work, unpaid. Worse still I had maimed my best friend / girlfriend and she wanted nothing to do with me as far as I could see. Did I mention bleak before? Well things were looking decidedly Dickensian now. Then I woke up.

My blood felt as if it was fizzing, I felt wonderful, I'm pretty sure I laughed. And I knew! I just knew that everything I had read about Jesus was true. I knew that He was the Son of God and that He was my Lord and Saviour. Nothing else mattered and I was sure, surer than I've ever been that He would see me alright. I told Jenni, then, on the advice of another Christian friend, I told my family to varying degrees of raised eyebrows. Then one Sunday I stood in front of Kennington Church and told them. They clapped! I now realise that I was being prayed for from the moment I set foot in the building. I was totally out of my depth and I realised that this was the place I needed to be, to learn, to grow and to be cared for in those first, sometimes dangerous, steps as a Christian.

Jenni and I married at that church in 2000: we somehow managed to pack in one hundred and fifty people into that odd wonderful place. As the years went on I became more and more involved, serving on the Church Council for three years, preaching on more than one occasion and generally mucking in when I was needed. I received the support and teaching as and when I needed it in a quite gentle way from a bewildering variety of people that is the hallmark of Kennington. I never felt preached at and in most cases never really realised that I was being taught.

As with all things there is a season for all things and when we moved away from the Kennington area we felt it was the right time to make the break from the church. Kennington Church had been such a major part of our lives over those years that leaving was just plain weird. And it continued to feel very odd for a long time afterwards. This must be a good testament to the love and respect that we felt for the church. A Christian needs solid teaching to make the move to other challenges. Kennington and the people there not only supplied that but offered unconditional love and friendship and I would like this chance to thank them for those things to both myself and my family.

Philip Osborne

My journey... the beginning

Church, whilst not an alien concept to me, was a very infrequent destination. It was something one had to do; family weddings and baptisms, and Parade services. Any sense of anything more, anything spiritual; any sense of God was non-existent to me. In fact such thoughts never crossed my mind.

Yes I was baptised as an infant, but I never attended Sunday school. Church and God were not part of my world or my thinking at all.

In March 1993 my first son was born. As a family we were living in Kennington, a suburb of Ashford, Kent. This was the area where my then wife, Helen, had grown up. As part of her growing up she had spent some time with the Sunday school at the Kennington UR/Methodist Church on Faversham Road, but had not been near nor by the church for some years.

Following our son's birth Helen noted that a new Parent and Toddler group had started at the church led by Jenny and Margaret, two members of the congregation, and Helen went along for company. The welcome was warm, and soon friendships blossomed. Before long Helen was encouraged to give a church service a try and was further drawn in by the warmth and love shown by all within the church congregation, as was our son and Helen's daughter.

After a few months the nagging started (at least I remember it as nagging, well what did I want to do with church!).

Quite often Helen and the children would be driven home after a service and there would be smiles and hugs and waves – all very nice!!

The nagging continued...

I eventually gave in. I was working a lot of hours at the time and time-off was precious to me; I really didn't want to spend it in a stuffy old church with do-gooders – I resented being there on the few occasions I did attend.

And what a barmy lot they appeared to be – there was a lot that was 'nice'; everyone was warm and friendly, but this wasn't the 'church' I knew. Charismatic is the word used to describe it. They had something, there was something about them, it was nothing I had ever seen or experienced before. It was weird! I was intrigued. These people seemed to know God as a present reality.

I attended the church on several occasions over the next few months, and for the most part I was rather uncomfortable with it all, I wasn't sure what I was doing there.

On one particular Sunday, 2nd January 1994, I went with my family to church. It was a day I didn't really want to be there. However, I found myself praying to God, "If

You really do exist, show me." I don't know what I was expecting but nothing happened. I left empty. Unusually I found myself at church again the following Sunday, two Sundays off was remarkable. I again said the prayer I had spoken the previous week. I left disappointed. The people around me seemed to experience God within the moment, I made no connection. It wasn't for me and in my thinking I was never going to come again.

During the following week I was able to secure a weekend off – nothing like being in the right place at the right time! Helen didn't want to go to church without me, but really wanted to go – I made an effort and went, but tried not to engage. I found myself praying that same prayer once more, almost laughing at myself. The worship leaders began singing 'Purify my heart'. Whether it was the angelic voices of Becci and Siobhan or I was hearing the singing of the angels I do not know but tears were streaming down my face.

I was burning hot and red as a beetroot – or so I was told later – and I was rooted to the chair. I could not move.

I felt surrounded by love and peace – simply saying it in that way does not express anything of the moment, I simply do not have the words to convey the sense of what I experienced in those moments.

Then, as I was held in that moment, so completely unaware and detached from everything and everyone in that place I felt something in my chest. So very lightly and so very tenderly I felt a touch on my heart, it grew. A moment later and I could feel fingertips on my heart and then my heart being held as if in a hand. I was overwhelmed by love such as I had never experienced. God knew me and revealed Himself to me, my irreverent prayer had been answered in a way I could never have imagined. In that moment I had been reborn.

As I became aware of my surroundings once again, I was aware of people around me, praying quietly, with hands upon my shoulders. I was led through a prayer of repentance and I gave my life to Jesus.

It was the 16th January 1994 and I was alive for the first time.

Rose Bowden

"When I Feel The Touch".......

I was born in Walworth, in London in 1924, the youngest of eight children. My father died when I was only three, leaving my mother to bring us up alone. To give herself some rest she sent us to Sunday School at the local church, where I learned the basic Bible stories (and enjoyed the sweets being handed out by the Sunday School Teacher).

As I grew up life was not easy, but we coped thanks to Mum working hard, and she built us into a strong family. I left school when I was fourteen and started work, just a year before war broke out. During the early part of the war I worked in the Sun Pat factory which was hit: I was blown across the floor, but a colleague ended up being blown into a vat of boiling oil. Being young I was scared and ran home. My mother then took me to her mother's home in Woking, where I worked making wireless sets for the military. Woking was much less targeted than London and, although there was still a blackout, there was a cinema and a fair we could go to.

After a while in Woking we moved back to London, living opposite the home where one of my sisters lived, and I started war work in another factory. One evening my mother called us all together and said she wanted us to go to the local school for the night and stay in the Air Raid Shelter there. When we came out next morning and went to our homes, my sister's home had received a direct hit, and our home was badly damaged – if Mum had not had the premonition, I would not have survived to tell the tale.

Following this bombing we moved out to Bedford, again staying with family, and I learned to drive a crane in an engineering factory, before we returned to London in 1943, and more engineering work in support of the war effort. One day, in my lunch time, I went into the pub next door to the factory and a soldier - who was home on leave - asked me for a dance: that was my Bill to whom I was married two years later, and with whom I enjoyed fifty four happy years of marriage. We married in church - Bill was from a Roman Catholic background but neither of us was `religious` at this time.

After the war Bill worked in London, then we moved to Bedford, eventually getting a caretaker's job with a tied cottage and a lot more room than we had previously had - but we were Londoners, so we moved back, finally ending up (after a few moves) in a flat in Peckham.

All this time one of my nieces had been going through a very difficult time in her marriage, and eventually suffered mental illness because of the strain she was under, ending up in a hospital because of it. She slowly recovered - throwing away all her medication - and met a spiritualist who tried to show her that this was the way to solve her problems. Fortunately she did not go along this path, but met a Christian who invited her to church where she 'fell in love with Jesus', and started to read the Bible from cover to cover, regularly praying for hours at a time. When she spoke to us about her new-found friend (Jesus) we saw the change in her, and her excitement, and we wanted a bit of what she had got.

Consequently, when she invited us to go with her to a Billy Graham meeting in 1989 (I was then aged sixty five) I would have jumped at the chance except that I suffered from fear of crowds, so would only go if I could have an aisle seat - which she arranged for me. After Cliff Richard had sung (a real bonus for me), Billy Graham gave his appeal and I eventually took Bill by the hand and we went forward together. When I reached the front the crowd seemed to disappear, I was no longer afraid of them, and I spent some time with a lady counsellor whilst a man was talking and praying with Bill.

We needed to find a church, which the Billy Graham organisation tried to help with, but the one from which the vicar came to see us was not for us – we just didn't fit in there. One day Bill saw a group of Christians outside, on the street, and he came home to me and said, "They are the ones we want to be with", so we joined the Barnabus church (one of the New Frontiers group) meeting in Sidcup, where we were made so welcome, and a lady called Barbara Stokes took us under her wing and, over a period of about six months, taught us about God and the Bible answering all our questions. Without Barbara I would not be where I am now.

We were baptised (fully immersed) whilst with that church, with all the children sitting round the baptistery pool, singing when we came out of the water. After our meeting with God we no longer wanted to go riding around the countryside on Bill's motorbike; there was another focus to our lives.

Although it was a wrench, we moved to one of the Icthus churches when Bill became ill, as it was much closer to home. One thing I loved was the excitement of the Marches for Jesus we were involved with, joining with lots of other Christians in the streets and parks, waving flags, singing hymns and choruses, being proud of our faith.

Bill soon became very ill, but never lost his faith in Jesus. God gave me the strength to cope with it all: it wasn't nice seeing my husband suffer as he did, although my Bill never was one to complain. The people in the church were a great support to me during that time, with his being in and out of hospital, and very weak.

Very shortly after Bill died in March 2000 I moved to Ashford, to be near my sister and my niece (Bill and I couldn't have children of our own), and I now have a lovely bungalow which suits me just right. After looking around at several other churches I came to Kennington URC/Methodist Church, and immediately felt wanted and welcomed, especially by Mavis Rodriguez. I feel very much at home here, and, although I miss the speaking in tongues during the services, there is a lot of love and care, and a lady like me is accepted for who I am. I am sure God led me here.

I still speak to my niece every week on the phone, and we pray for each other; for several years we went to Ashburnham Place together for a short retreat – to meet with God in a place of peace and harmony, where people from many nations would come together for fellowship and prayer – a real foretaste of heaven.

God has been good to me, He protected us during the war and provided me with a wonderful marriage. If you were to ask me how my life would be without God I would say that I would be a lonely old lady with nothing to look forward to, but God has also provided friends, strength and a hope – no, a certainty – for what lies ahead.

Joan Fidler ═══════════════════

When Ted and I were married in Dulwich we were church-goers, although neither of us was from a church-going family. I had been sent to Sunday School as a child, like most of my contemporaries because, "that is what everyone did" in those days. I had never doubted that there was a God, I just didn't know Him for myself, and it could easily have stayed that way. When he was young my son, Gary, made a friend at school and I got to know the mother – short skirted, very lively, and when I found out she was a Methodist Minister's wife I was amazed – that didn't seem like the experience of church that I had had until that time.

Ted and I went round to the manse on many occasions, and found the minister and his wife to be perfectly normal people – even to the extent of Ted sharing a few cans of beer with the husband! We were slowly drawn into the life of the church in Brixton Hill, and when we moved to Ashford in 1964 the Methodist tradition of 'linking' with a church in your new destination meant we found a ready home in Bank Street Church. This was quite a distance for us, and when we realised that Kennington Church was in walking distance we transferred there – fortunately they had evening services which meant that we could go off camping from Friday night to Sunday afternoon, and be back in time for the evening service!

With friends from Kennington Church (and others) we went to Spring Harvest in Minehead in 1985 and 1986, and whilst we were there a group of men prayed for Ted at the 'Prayer Mountain'. Ted was a wonderful gentleman (even if I am biased). He never thought too much of himself, and never pushed himself forward, hanging back almost out of wishing to avoid any limelight, or maybe he was unsure of what full commitment might mean. We had wondered if there was anything we could usefully do for God (Ted was an electrician, I worked as an administrator at the local hospital), but had no idea what we could offer. One day we found the 'Mission Area' with all the potential roles that mission organisations needed filling, which made us realise we had something God could use. Although it took some years before we actually stepped out in faith, Spring Harvest was a real 'launch pad' for Ted.

During the 1980s I was baptised with some other members of Kennington, where I spoke of an experience that convinced me that God was God, and that He loved ME! I had become friendly with a lady (Theresa) from the local Roman Catholic Church who encouraged us to go on a Marriage Encounter Weekend and, after a couple of years of this encouragement, we succumbed. With around nine other couples, several Roman Catholic priests and a handful of nuns we arrived for the weekend feeling very nervous and uncertain; by the end of the weekend we were just bathed in love! On the Sunday afternoon the ladies were asked to write a love letter, either to their husbands or to God, and as I sat there in my room, not knowing what to write, I heard God say "This is My kind of love, make a choice"; I have never looked back since then. Although we were not part of their church, on our return the Catholic fellowship held a party for us to celebrate our weekend; we were overwhelmed. There were regular follow up meetings for those who had been on the Marriage Encounter Weekends, and at one weekend in Canterbury we were so 'swept up in God' that we said, "Here we are, send us!" Little did we know!!

After some of the folk at Kennington left the fellowship we settled in Ashford Christian Fellowship (ACF), under the inspired, and inspiring, leadership of Syd and Liz Doyle, who not only encouraged us to look outward, they also prophesied that we would travel. Missionary work runs deep in the DNA of ACF and one week we had a lady missionary speaking about her trust in God to provide, and how He never let her down - but I was not ready for the big step of faith. We did join Syd and Liz, and others, on a two week trip to Romania in 1990 which was very emotional: it was soon after the fall of Ceauşescu, and people were openly declaring their faith in Jesus after many years of suppression. When I look back at our time in Romania, God was preparing us for what lay ahead.

Ted had become very unhappy in his work, and decided to leave - on one camping weekend he wrote out his letter of resignation and sent it off. I asked him what he wanted to do to fill his time - Ted was not one to sit around and do nothing - to which he replied, "I'd like a little driving job, nothing heavy", so we prayed about it. Soon afterwards I was having coffee with one of my colleagues at work and mentioned that Ted had resigned, and then the conversation moved on to other matters: several days later she said, "I hope you don't mind my asking, but my son wants someone to do a little driving job for his pet shop in Ashford, would Ted be offended if he was asked?"

Our son and family had moved away, and our grandchildren lived eighty miles from us, so we took the decision to sell up and move - but houses were sticking and nothing happened for eighteen months. Ted and I had recently had operations, and were both off work, so we decided to go to the Estate Agents to find out prospects for a sale, only to find the place boarded up - it had closed and nobody told us! We didn't readvertise the house so when, some eighteen months later we had a phone call asking `is your house still up for sale` we were a bit surprised - the man who rang had just bought the old Estate Agents and found our advert in the back of a filing cabinet he was throwing out. He was calling his new Estate Agents "Way Out", and we wondered, "Is this our way out?" - and it was. He came round the next day to look at the place, offered to do the sale for a greatly reduced commission, and within three weeks we had a buyer, who had no chain, and wanted a quick sale!

On the day we handed the keys over to the new owners I left my job in the hospital, and we moved in to our caravan (parked on a friend's drive). The next day we flew to North Carolina with Paul and Shirley Langford for a six week holiday, meeting up with Tom Lyons (an American pastor who had developed close links with Kennington Church). During our last week in Carolina when Tom asked us what we really wanted to do we said, "To travel, and serve God!" In his normal style Tom replied, "Let's pray about that and give it to God", and after we did so he said, "Now it is in God's hands."

Whilst we were in America I heard God say to me, "You are not to go home and buy another house" – which I found rather strange, but kept it to myself as I thought Ted would have considered me 'peculiar' if I told him. When I plucked up the courage to tell him, he just looked at me and said, "You too?" He had been given the same message.

On our return to Ashford I went to take some photos of our holiday to show the Estate Agent only to find that the place was, again, boarded up! How many houses could he have sold in that short time? We maintain that it was an angel that sold our house.

When we settled back into living in Ashford (in our caravan – all those years of camping had prepared us for this nomadic lifestyle) we continued worshipping with ACF. Ted began to use his practical skills to help renovate premises to be used for a youth centre, and I started accompanying the leadership team on pastoral visiting, as well as being involved in the administration of the church. This included preparing the hall for regular Thursday coffee mornings which would involve a speaker, booked well in advance. On one particular Thursday a lady named Val Smith from Youth With A Mission (YWAM) came to speak – I had never heard about YWAM but when she was speaking my heart leapt, it seemed so right.

Afterwards I spoke to her and said, "Ted and I have retired, we have sold our home," to which she replied, "And you want to join in with us". So in 1991 we went to investigate YWAM, and they to investigate us, and so began twenty amazing, exciting, fulfilling years of travel, serving God in countries around the globe.

In these twenty years we saw blind people receive their sight when serving on the Mercy ships, we were able to comfort the dying AIDS patients and to show compassion to the bar girls and prostitutes in Thailand among many other blessings. Ted's practical skills came to the fore whilst building orphanages in Africa, and in so many other ways all our life experiences and our abilities were put to good use: God never wastes anything that is given over to Him, and He does give us the desires of our hearts!

Janet Dray

I spent several years at the Kennington United Reformed / Methodist Church – in fact it was my spiritual birth place, and was the spiritual 'home' in which I was nurtured in the Christian faith. Just as the first few years of a natural child's life are crucial to development, those early years as a Christian are vital for growth and grounding in the new life the individual has been born into. I will always be grateful to this fellowship (many of the precious people now departed and with the Lord) for the love, the teaching, the opportunity to develop gifting – and even to make mistakes and get back on my feet again – and much more besides.

I was brought up in a Christian home. As a family we were regular church attendees and I automatically thought I was a Christian, and called myself one. The Christianity I knew kept me from much waywardness, but it was very legalistically based – all do's and don'ts – little about relationship to the Saviour, nor on the power of the Word, and nor did I experience the joy of true fellowship.

As the years went by I maintained my "Christian" lifestyle well into my twenties. Then I met and married a man who was much into Buddhism – and I too became involved.

Life became very bleak – in fact dark – and I increasingly became riddled with fear. Deep inside. I believe I knew that I was not living in the truth, but would never have admitted this fact.

I came to Kennington, recently divorced and wanting a fresh start. I had a new job and was now living in a new area – but soon after I became quite ill with Glandular Fever. As I was recovering, through my mother staying with me and attending the Kennington United Reformed/Methodist Church I became linked back to Christianity. In this warm fellowship I found "real people" – people who shared with one another, studied the Word together, and met outside regular church hours, and people who were interested in me as a person. It was in this loving environment that God moved in my life and I was born again, and God began to put my life back together again. I had never before experienced such love, trust and joy – I now knew the meaning of being brothers and sisters in Christ.

I also want to say that it was in this church God brought into my life Chris – who became my beloved husband, and we have been blessed with two wonderful daughters, now grown up.

Whilst I was recovering from my Glandular Fever, and was very weak and unable to participate in much of the church life, a lady come over from America, the sister of one of the members of the church, who had never met me or heard about my illness. When she was met at the airport she said, "There is a lady I have to pray with", and described me and my symptoms perfectly.

On the Sunday afternoon a few days after arriving she, and some ladies from within the fellowship, came to my home and prayed for me, anointing the top of my head with oil for healing. Those present tell me that the colour came back into my face from the top of my head downwards, as opposed to the normal way of the colour rising with the flow of blood, upwards from the torso. As the colour came back so did my strength, and I was well enough to walk to church that evening and tell everyone what had happened, and I have not looked back since.

When our first daughter was very small, God told us to move from the Kennington United Reformed/Methodist Church. We took a while to be obedient, not wanting to leave, but we eventually did so, and it was painful. Since that time we have been in four different fellowships. It has been only relatively recently, as we look back, that we can see how it has been God's purpose to move us around -as He has been teaching us, by experience, much about church life. He has also instructed us in His truths and taught us about who we are "in Him" – this has been through many teachers as well as "knocks" – and it has all helped us grow in our spiritual walk.

Now we have reached retirement years (as the natural world terms it!) we believe we are more prepared to use all that God has taught us in these past three decades to help other Christians grow in the faith.

Joe and Jenny Kavanagh ▬

We both spent our early years in London and started going out together when Jenny was sixteen and Joe was eighteen, marrying some four years later in 1973. We were married in a Registry Office because we were from different backgrounds – Joe from an Irish Catholic family, and Jenny from an English Protestant family. In Joe's case the family were regular church-goers (his father having served as an altar boy in his youth), and Joe having attended a Catholic School, whilst Jenny's parents attended on high days and holidays, and when Jenny was involved in plays or other activities at the church. With this difference between our families the course of least resistance was to marry on neutral territory. Despite this, there were some tensions both within and between our families, and so we were advised to move away from London, so we moved to Ashford in the same year as we married. Joe had already found a job there before our wedding.

Although we both had some Christian background, Sunday School, Youth Group, and the Catholic School education, by the time we married God was not on the scene, and that continued for a while after we had moved down to Ashford. Initially we lived in a small cottage in Sellinge, then moved into Stanhope before buying our first home in Grosvenor Road, Kennington in 1976, which is where things took off.

We have been blessed with two daughters, Becci (born in 1976) and Siobhan (born in 1979), but one of our big regrets is that Jenny's father died in 1980, and so had very little chance to see his grandchildren. When he died suddenly this really affected Jenny, causing her to become withdrawn and very angry with the God she knew existed, but with whom she had had no relationship or communication for years. This feeling of "It is unfair" kept nagging away, as did the questions about life and death. There were also the regrets about the things left unsaid which we know everyone has, but when it becomes personal, it is difficult to accept you are not unique, and this is hard to handle.

Joe, meanwhile, was becoming more dependent upon alcohol to boost his confidence. Alcohol had always played a big part in his family, with some members unable to control their need for it, and the concern whether Joe was heading down that path, allied to Jenny's feelings following her father's death, started to cause some friction in the home.

One day Don Collins (whose wife, May, appears elsewhere in this book) knocked on our door accompanied by an American evangelist, and started to share a few things with Joe, as Jenny was otherwise occupied. Joe had the opinion that Jesus was a 'good man', a 'hero', but that was all. Don was not one to be discouraged, however, and made many more visits to our home over the following weeks, finally inviting us to visit the Kennington United Reformed/ Methodist Church, which Jenny did. Joe took a rather different approach – whenever he saw Don Collins coming up the garden path he would hop over the back fence and go to the local pub! On one such occasion, whilst sitting in the pub, pint in hand, Joe wondered why he was willing to take anyone on in a fight, or argument, but this old man – who he could easily have flattened – could drive him out of his own home.

At the church the welcome, the love and the joy seen in so many people was so attractive that Jenny and the girls soon became regular attendees, and the fellowship were praying for Joe. Sundays soon spilled over into midweek Bible studies and meetings, as Jenny wanted in her life what the people in the church 'up the road' obviously had in theirs.

In 1987 Phyllis Hull asked if we wanted to go to Spring Harvest – a Christian week held in Butlins in Minehead (among other places): this was a problem as we would only go as a family, and Joe was not keen (to put it tactfully), but he agreed we would go and he would attend one meeting during the week. In the company of many others from the church we loaded up our car, and drove to Minehead, to be greeted by thousands of happy, smiling, praising Christians. Once we unpacked, and had sorted out what meeting Jenny and the girls were to go to that evening, Joe went back to the car to drive off site and find a pub. The car would not start, no matter what Joe (who is an engineer) tried, and despite asking for a tow around the car park it refused to start – so he walked to the pub, followed by another engineer from where he worked – and spent the evening fending off questions about Spring Harvest from interested locals.

The car steadfastly refused to start all week, unless we were going off site as a family, in which case it worked perfectly. Joe kept his promise and came to a morning meeting in the Big Top where, as part of the meeting, we were asked to gather in groups of three to pray for Saltmine (a theatre company). This was a problem as Jenny was not used to praying out loud, and Joe was not going to be a hypocrite and say what he did not believe. He also suffered from a severe stutter which made speaking in front of others a serious problem. The lady who made up our triplet was wonderful – she said she would do all the praying, not for Saltmine, but for us as a couple, and for our family, that God's love would enfold us and this love would cast out any fears we had. Joe was more emotional then than at any time in our marriage up to that point.

At the end of that week, on Good Friday, April 17 1987, in the Big Top, Jenny saw Jesus with his arms open, calling her. There was a hesitation as we were a couple, and there was a worry about Joe being abandoned or left behind, but Jesus said "I'll look after Joe", Jenny was then overwhelmed by love and peace, and had this inner certainty that when Jesus said He would look after Joe, He meant it.

On our return to Ashford members of the church were sharing experiences of Spring Harvest and agreed that we should ask God to put a time limit on Joe finding his own faith, and agreed that six months was a reasonable timescale. Joe was oblivious of this, having put his Minehead experience behind him as "an emotional reaction". He was, however, starting to look at himself 'from the outside' and seeing the hard, prickly, tense person he was becoming: this was brought home to him when he went to ruffle his daughter's hair, and she flinched – as if expecting her father to hit her.

Three months later, one Monday Joe went for a walk one lunchtime, and sat down by the river near his work, and said, through the tears, "If there is a God, You'd better come into my life and sort me out as I've made a real mess of it myself" – then went back to work. We learned then, never to set God a challenge like that!

That night when we were asleep, Joe was woken up and saw a small spot of light, which grew to resemble a miniature sun with rays coming from the edges, which grew steadily brighter until it filled the whole room, so that the room was too bright to enable him to see anything – and Jenny stayed asleep! Although he could not make out anything due to the intensity of the light, Joe heard a voice speaking in a language he could not understand (but now knows to be Aramaic) and felt a power as if he was holding an electric power cable and the surge of electricity was running through him, and over him, but he was not being burnt. Slowly he could see figures with white robes, edged in black, emerging from the light, but could not make out their faces, and these figures came and stood either side of him. Whilst he lay still he was comfortable, but if he tried to sit up or climb out of bed he was pressed down by a power he could not resist.

Slowly the light started to dim, the figures faded, and eventually the light receded to a small spot, then went out.

Jenny stayed asleep but Joe lay there, confused, and with legs like jelly.

Somehow Joe went to work the next day, and said nothing to Jenny – how could he explain what he had experienced? On the Thursday, three days later, Jenny was ironing, and was listening to a tape of the last sermon given at Kennington by Richard Burgess. After the sermon Richard seemed to have stepped back from the microphone and spoken in tongues. Joe shouted, "That's the language" and then explained to Jenny all he had seen, heard and experienced on the Monday night. On impulse he opened a Bible, and it opened at Acts 9 – the conversion of Saul of Tarsus. Whilst he has never put himself in the same league as the apostle, Joe was able to see how his experience had been in the same vein as that of St Paul, even down to the three days interval.

After this, we went to church as a family, and met up with Paul Langford (another engineer from the same factory, who had also had a wonderful encounter with God whilst visiting his family in America.) There was still a reluctance to make a full commitment, something was holding Joe back, and that something was broken on the 2nd of November. Paul Langford's sister (Jay Bird) had come over from America and prayed for him, and told him three things: firstly was something that nobody else knew, even Jenny, (the details of which are not relevant here), secondly that he had a lump in his stomach which would be cured, and thirdly that his stammer would be cured. Joe went down under the power of the Spirit, and, when he came round, the pain of the 'hidden secret' had gone, as had the lump, and as had his stammer. So started Joe's walk with the Lord which led him into leadership in Kennington, and led us into other fellowships, from where we have come full circle and are currently worshipping again at the United Reformed/ Methodist Church which, although smaller than of old, is where God wants us to be at the moment.

Soon after Joe took his step of faith we dedicated our children to God, and made the vows to each other that we would have made if we had married in church: this seemed a natural step to be reaffirmed in the eyes of God now that we were united in God.

Signs and wonders follow those who believe, as it says in the Bible. The following summer we went across Europe to see Joe's brother, who was an alcoholic, but would not admit it, and prayed with him, although he did not accept his need for prayer. Sometime later, after we had returned to England, he was arrested after being involved in an accident where he was at fault through drink, and we had a phone call from his wife. We prayed, and the next day we heard that a priest had visited him in prison with the news that he would be released if he would go to a clinic to help him dry out: that was twenty years ago and he has not touched a drop since, and the part alcohol plays in all of Joe's family has drastically reduced.

We have also prayed for other members of our families, friends and work colleagues, and seen healings from cancer and other illnesses; and it is not only people who respond to prayer. There was one occasion at work when Joe was on night shift, as the only engineer, and he was given a machine to try to mend that all the day shift engineers had failed to repair and the company had sent to America for an expert to come over. Joe prayed, laid hands on the machine, pressed the 'start' button, and off it went! He had to fill in the Engineering Log Book, and the entry was read out by his manager in the Management Morning Meeting "As others had tried and failed to start this machine, I laid hands on it, and prayed that in the name of Jesus it would be healed and start": Joe was not popular!

This latter event took place when the company had decided to rejig the engineering shifts, and Joe had been allocated permanent nights – which was not conducive to good family life, and which we felt to be manifestly unfair. During an interview with the factory manager, Joe was basically given no option but to stay on nights, or to fight it through the Trade Union of which he has been an active member for many years. Despite many colleagues expecting him to bring the Union on board Joe was reminded of when his Biblical namesake, Joseph, was set up by Pottiphar's wife, and God honoured him in the long run, so Joe accepted his position. To cut a long story short, after a few years Joe was restored to normal shifts, with a pay rise and a bonus, his reputation was enhanced among the site management, and all the managers who had tried to keep him on permanent nights were moved out from the factory. As part of this process all the engineers had to take tests, and Joe, despite not being academic or particularly confident with computers, scored the highest marks.

Outside of work we have seen many simple, everyday answers to prayer – one final example to finish with: we were involved in a house group and had just finished the study book we had been following, so needed a further topic to study as a group. We were in our home, talking and praying about this, among other things, when there was a knock on our door. The son of a family at one of our sister churches (Bank Street) was down in Kent, visiting his parents, and had been sitting outside our home with the study book "The Way of the Spirit" in his car when he felt God was saying, "See that house there, take the book and give it to them." He was obedient, and had let God direct his steps, which is what we want to do from now on.

Richard and Pam Burgess

Having recently moved house in 1984, God led us with two young children, Timothy and Lisa, to join the United Reformed Methodist Church in Kennington – our third child Deborah was born a year later in 1985. In fact we hadn't long moved in when we had two visits, one from May Collins, and the other from Alf Hart, asking us to consider coming to the church – how the Christian grapevine works, combined with God's purpose!

We came from quite a different background (both being brought up as Strict Baptists then becoming Christians in a Pentecostal Church), and God was leading us on a journey. At the United Reformed / Methodist Church we discovered a body of people from a variety of backgrounds who believed in and loved Jesus, were united in the Spirit and committed to knowing, seeking and serving Him. From the moment we arrived we were made to feel at home by the people's love and friendliness.

God was at work building His church, and one of the important elements to that were the all night prayer meetings which were held from time to time, where we would gather in the lounge for an extended period of worshipping and seeking God and fellowship with one another, ending with breakfast and Communion – they were precious times.

Some of the times we remember were visits from a team from Roffey Place, where Colin Urquhart's influential ministry was based, another was the visit of Marilyn Baker the blind singer-songwriter. A number of us also went to the Queens Park Rangers football ground for the visit of Luis Palau and to the annual Spring Harvest Christian event at Prestatyn. We also got involved with local mission through events like the Billy Graham Livelink.

Having some experience of ministry in music and word it wasn't long before Richard Davis asked me (Richard) to be involved in different aspects of ministry in the church, ultimately joining the Eldership, where we enjoyed some good fellowship together in the oversight of the church.

It was a joy to see people coming to know Christ as their Lord and Saviour, and being baptised in water – we used to borrow a portable baptistry and set it up in the back of the hall. They were always great occasions full of the joy of the Lord. I remember one occasion where I was involved in baptising someone taller than myself and nearly got pulled under as well!

It was also great to see people growing and flourishing in Christ, and the body worshipping in Spirit and in truth, knowing the presence and power of God through His Spirit at work among us.

We remember those times down at the home of Don and May Collins, worshipping together on the 'island' in their garden. I (Richard) remember going with Don Collins, who had a passion to reach others, into the local pub to share the gospel from time to time on a Friday evening. Through the encouragement of Richard Davis it also provided a place for my own personal growth and development in ministry. When Richard married and moved on John Lakin (the Methodist Superintendent) was happy for Janet Huang (who later became Janet Dray) and myself to continue the oversight of the church.

We highly value the time we spent at Kennington United Reformed / Methodist Church, and have since gone on to lead and minister in two churches, with occasional ministry trips to Romania, Kenya and the Democratic Republic of Congo. Recently I (Richard), following God's leading, have overseen the merger of one church with another, and we both continue to be actively involved in the life and ministry of the church.

Jane Burnham

I can't remember a time when I did not believe in the existence of God, but my understanding of who He is was very inadequate.

I was taken or sent to Sunday School from an early age, but can remember no specific lessons learned. Young children were taken out to the rectory during the sermon. Older children had a short talk from the Rector at the end of the service. I came away from those sessions with an awareness that God cared about me, and that He was available to me through prayer. I also loved Mr. Reece's Welsh accent.

When Mr. Reece retired the village church was joined with three others, which meant we no longer had weekly services. Even when there were services there was no Sunday School, so it was easy to stop going to church. I took to fishing in the local lake instead.

I never had a great relationship with my mother. She frequently let me know that I was a great disappointment to her. She had lost her father when she was only three and was devoted to her mother. I was very much a 'Daddy's girl'.

I loved to be out in the garden with him, and later going round the farm where he worked, especially at lambing time. Dad was a quiet man but let me know he liked my company. He also drove myself and my friends to Girl Guides meetings in a nearby village.

At the age of twelve life went seriously wrong for me. After a short illness my father died. This was the beginning of a time of extreme loneliness. I had had two friends who lived on farms at either end of the village. For various reasons they had never liked each other. Circumstances changed to bring them together at the same school where they became friends and gradually I was left out of their plans and activities. I had already had to stop going to Guides because there was no-one able or willing to take me.

I went to a different school to the others, where I had one remaining close friend. At the end of the summer term, when I was fourteen, she had told me about her new boyfriend.

Just a week or so into the holiday my brother held a party in a pub in the local town to celebrate his birthday and leaving school. My mother bribed me to say I wanted to go so my eldest brother would take us in his car. She was afraid my other brother would get drunk and crash his motor bike.

After what seemed like ages being very bored (I knew hardly anyone and they were all older than me) a nice young man asked me to dance and I spent the rest of the evening with him. It only occurred to me to ask his name at the very end when the disco had finished and we were waiting for my eldest brother to take us home. Horror! He was my best friend's new boyfriend!

I spent the rest of the summer 'fishing' but more often just staring at the water, or walking our dog until I found a gate or old tree stump to sit on, and sitting, wishing I was dead. We still had in the house a shoe box full of part used medicines from my father's illness and I often thought about taking some to commit suicide. I was saved on this occasion by the dog. I could not think of how or where I could go and not be given away by him. I almost never left the house without taking him with me so to leave him behind would instantly be suspicious. If I took him I couldn't face the thought either of abandoning him somewhere where he might not be found or cause me to be found too soon.

So at the end of the summer I went back to school still alive to face my friend. My brother had very considerately given her a full account of the party.

After the long hot summer the first day back at school was pouring with rain so we all had to stay inside at lunch time. We were supposed to go to our form rooms, which put me in the uncomfortable position of being in the same room as my friend, with others wondering why we were not speaking to one another.

At this time I was a terrible gossip. I had a network of 'contacts' through whom I could find out something about almost anyone in time. But there was one boy who intrigued me. He waited at the same bus stop as me but unlike my older school friends, who would not acknowledge they knew me before their friends, he would happily talk to even the youngest pupils waiting there. I had pointed him out to my usual contacts but they had been unable even to tell me his name.

While I was sitting feeling thoroughly miserable that wet day a girl, who had come as a new pupil right at the end of the last term, came and asked if I would like to go to the Christian Fellowship meeting with her. I agreed. Anything to get out of the room I was in!

However I very quickly began to have second thoughts! I was on the verge of leaving when in walked my mystery boy, who also had a lovely Welsh accent, so I stayed.

The person leading the meeting that week drew a picture as she talked illustrating the verses,' Enter through the narrow gate. For wide is the gate and broad is the road that leads to destruction, and many enter through it. But small is the gate and narrow the road that leads to life, and only a few find it'. Matthew 7:13,14. I left that meeting knowing I had to find that narrow way.

The Christian fellowship would have special meetings at weekends. Just a few weeks later a walk was organised with tea at one of the teachers' homes. The walk was rained off but we met and played games, most with some sort of Christian basis. During that time I felt very odd. I can only describe it as feeling as if I was in a glass bubble. I was in the room with the others but somehow not included. The day ended with a Bible study on John 15. When we got to where it says, 'You are My friends if you do what I command' in v15, God was speaking directly to me. Here was the answer to my loneliness.

I still had several more steps to take before I fully realised the true relationship God wants to have with us all. After this meeting I bought a modern translation of the Bible and began to read it, along with the 'helps' from the Gideon's New Testament I had been given when I started at the grammar school. Another time when visiting a church attended by some of the others I was given an understanding of the work of the Holy Spirit and went forward for prayer to confess Jesus as my Lord and to receive the Spirit. The final stage at this time in my life was a celebration held in the Royal Albert Hall where I and others felt we had been given a foretaste of worship in heaven. I will never forget, as we drove away in our mini-bus all singing and hearing the song going out with the crowd of people as they left to go home.

But life at home was still hard. By the time I came to university I had become disillusioned and this seemed a good time to give up 'this God business'. God had other ideas. I had taken my Bible with me because I knew I would get snide comments from my mother if she saw I had left it behind. I was unpacking when my room neighbour came in, saw it in my hand and said,' Oh, are you a Christian too?' What could I say!

For the rest of my life I have found that Jesus is a friend indeed. I cannot give stories of great miracles as some can, but God has given me people to help and guide me as I have needed them, including the person who was to become my husband at the time my mother was dying from cancer. When our son was born gifts arrived just when they were needed. When Hugh and I went through a bad patch forgiveness and healing were only a prayer away.

At Kennington I became Sunday school teacher for several years, finding my faith both strengthened and challenged as I sought to make the Christian message understandable to a constantly changing group of children. Now I wait to see what God will call me to do next.

The title of this book is 'The Little Church Of Mended People'. I don't feel I am fully mended yet. Writing this has brought to the light the need to forgive people from my past. Yet I am confident that my friend Jesus will be with me and give me who and what I need to follow Him.

Rodney Wood

I remember a URC General Assembly at St George's Crowstone in Southend and being up in the back of the gallery. In the worship we were singing 'Hark what a sound, and too divine for hearing' (number 236 in Hymns and Psalms – though of course we were using Rejoice and Sing!) It was when we came to the last verse, that for a vivid moment I felt myself to be no longer in Southend – I had passed beyond this life – 'passed away' you might say. And yet I was not yet in that "Life after life after death" as N T Wright puts it, but in a place of waiting, waiting for a door to be opened.

At the same time I was singing with every fibre of my faith and being the words of that last verse:

Through life and death, through sorrow and through sinning,
He shall suffice me, for He hath sufficed.
Christ is the end, for Christ is the beginning,
Christ the beginning for the end is Christ.

Naturally, F W H Myers' hymn has been ever afterwards a very special hymn for me.

Paul and Shirley Langford

"Our walk"

We first met when I was fourteen, I moved into a house next door to Paul's grandmother, and Paul was living there at the time. I saw him riding down the street, backwards, on the handlebar of his bike and I thought, "What a show off!" It was certainly not love at first sight. If only I had known what God had in store for us! Forty three years of marriage.

We married when we were both twenty four, so I had known Paul for ten years, a long time by today's standards. We had two children; Nikki and Vincent. Life seemed happy, complete and settled. Although we had both been brought up nominally as Christians – we both went to Church schools and to Sunday School (I sang in the choir for a short time at Church before my lack of singing voice relegated me to ringing the bells) – neither of us had a 'living' faith.

Paul was a GI baby and lost touch with his father when he returned home to North Carolina. Letters to Paul were intercepted and not found until after his grandmother's death, so Paul had no idea that his father had been trying to contact him for many years. Paul went to North Carolina to meet his father and the family over there: I stayed behind with the children in case things did not go too well, but there was mutual love, and respect, and so a trip was planned for the following year for all of us to go 'over the pond'.

While in America we met up with his half sister (Jay Bird), and with a very gentle preacher, Tom Lyons. We spent many hours arguing about the Christian faith with them, trying to convince them they were wrong in their beliefs, but instead we became more and more convinced that God and the Bible were true, and decided we should, as a family, be baptised in the French Broad River.

On our return to the UK, as we had both been brought up as nominal Anglicans we started out for the local Anglican Church one Sunday evening, but as we were passing the Kennington United Reformed / Methodist Church we saw there was a service and I said "I don't know why but I think this is where we should go." On entering the church, there was a lovely atmosphere, and when the Peace was shared Gwen French stood on a chair to share the Peace with Paul (five feet nothing against six foot seven inches!), which broke the ice for all of us.

We continued attending the Church, visiting America many times – we were very tempted to move there as the American family offered us so much, but Paul's ill health made it impossible.

On many occasions Paul was convinced that God was talking to him and helping him through operations which were in their infancy in this country. Many times I sat on a chair in the hospital to be told I should be prepared for the worst. In fact there was one unique operation which was performed at a specialist hospital in London which had not previously been done in this country (and was reported in The Lancet). Paul told me that as he laid in bed the night before the operation he had an out of body experience, and heard a voice saying, "You will be fine, and will be out of hospital in six weeks", even though the consultant had told us it would be three months, if ever. The same voice also helped Paul through periods of intense pain following the operation: at one stage he shouted, "Take me, God, I've had enough", only for the reply, "You will be out in six weeks". The voice was right; Paul was transferred to Hammersmith Hospital, and then discharged six weeks to the day after the operation.

We were blessed with a big house, which became the base for the Church to meet for prayer and worship, often till the early hours of the morning, with many of the gifts of the Spirit being exercised, people becoming convicted, and people being healed. This is how the church started in the Acts of Apostles, and here it was, two thousand years later being re-enacted in Kennington. Tom Lyons visited on many occasions, from North Carolina, and brought with him a variety of ministers and teachers who have remained inspirational friends to many Christians for many years.

One evening which particularly sticks in my memory concerned a young man who was very ill in hospital. Joan Fidler was on duty at the hospital that evening, and rang through to ask if we would pray for this young man who was on the verge of death. Paul immediately volunteered to act as a 'proxy' point of prayer, so we laid hands on Paul and prayed for this lad. Later that evening we had a call from Joan to say that the young man had come back from the point of death. Two weeks later the young man walked into our service on the Sunday to thank us for praying for him. As soon as he saw Paul he spoke to him by name to thank him. When Paul asked how he knew his name the young man said, "I saw them laying hands on you."

Paul's health was fine for a few years and then the pituitary tumour came back. He had to go through the operation twice more within a year – nobody expected him to survive the second, let alone the third operation, but he did. Just before the third operation Paul told me he said to God, "You will let everybody down who has been praying for me if I die, and they won't believe" Paul survived, the hospital called it a miracle. God had answered his prayers.

Paul could listen to, and respond to God in ways that some of us cannot. One evening various members of Kennington Church were giving a concert at a local home for the elderly: most were telling jokes, reciting poetry or playing musical instruments and singing. When it came to Paul's turn, he sat there with his guitar on his lap, and for fifteen minutes talked about his time in hospital when he had a particularly unpleasant operation. Although people were crying with laughter, I did not think it appropriate for the evening (or the audience). How wrong I was! Afterwards one resident said that she was facing the same operation in the next couple of days and had been afraid, but Paul had put her mind at rest: he had obviously been guided by the God in whom he trusted.

When Vincent, who was away at University, was taken in his sleep at the age of twenty it was such a massive blow to all of us of us. Paul never lost his faith, he was always sure that God was looking after us and that He knew best. As for me I had a very hard time, as did my daughter Nikki, and it took us many months and years for us to agree with Paul that God knows best.

Nikki, her husband Mark and our then three grandchildren (there are now six grandchildren) wanted to live the dream we never could and emigrate to North Carolina. Despite his many health problems Paul had to go to North Carolina to facilitate their emigration as he was an American Citizen. Whilst over there he contacted food poisoning which, due to mishandling by the doctors, caused further complications and his health deteriorated.

We were now in a situation with no family around us, and a big lonely house, so we decided that we should do something as we had been blessed with so much. We had always said that we owned nothing, everything we had was given to us by God and we should use it to help people. Initially we opened our home to young lads from Iran and, when they left, to young people referred to us by Social Services. Sometimes we had as many as three of them in the house at any one time along with their numerous mates, so the house was very full and lively again. Many of these young people had never had love in their lives or someone to care for them. We both cared very much for them through the good and the very, very bad times, and planted seeds of

God's love in their lives which – with time – we hope will fruit.

When Paul suddenly taken into hospital in January 2012 we were told that his aneurisium was leaking and there was nothing that could be done. I cried and cried: I said, "Paul, I cannot live without you. How will I cope?" – Paul's last words to me – which I will always treasure – were, "This is God's will, I am not scared. I know where I am going and you will be alright. People will look after you". Paul died in his sleep peacefully some hours later with me asleep by his side.

Omid and Hafi, the first two who came to us, were certainly a blessing from God – they have been like sons, literally, both before Paul's death, and since. They have helped Paul's words come true. I have also been supported, and loved, more than I could have expected. There is a big gap in my life, but these two lads, family and friends, are there for me, and my God, in whom Paul never lost faith, has plans for me. What they are I am not sure but I am waiting.

Lightning Source UK Ltd.
Milton Keynes UK
UKOW050153131012

200524UK00005B/1/P